Great Parenting Skills

For Navigating Your Kid's Personality

Seems like a good book to help parents & grand-parents deal with a child's personality in a positive way.

Kate Jones, M.Ed.
Wayne Jones, M.Ed.

Published by:
Career/LifeSkills Resources Inc.
Concord, ON L4K 2M2
www.clsr.ca

Cover Art By: Barb Kwolek - www.barbkwolekdesigns.com

Author Photos By: Michael Hewis - www.hewisphoto.com

Library and Archives Canada Cataloguing in Publication

Jones, Kate, 1951-, author
Great parenting skills for navigating your kids personality
/ Kate Jones, M.Ed., Wayne Jones, M.Ed.

Includes bibliographic references.
ISBN 978-1-894422-55-0 (pbk.)

1. Parenting. I. Jones, Wayne, 1949-, author II. Title.

HQ755.8.J65 2015   649.1   C2014-908505-2

We would like to dedicate this book to our own family – our inspiration, and our source of many anecdotes and stories you will encounter here. Our parenting journey with our own daughters, Becky and Laural, was filled with lots of joy, some tears, and yes, much learning. The expansion of our family, including sons-in-law (Steve and Mike) and four grandchildren (Kyla, Paige, Matthew and Chloe) continues to shape our understanding of human nature and temperament as we enjoy rich experiences together. Through our many shared holidays, family traditions, and day-to-day interactions, we now enjoy a journey filled with learning and growing as an extended family with diverse personalities.

Acknowledgements

In addition to learning from our own extended family members, we want to acknowledge the parents, guardians and grandparents in our many parent workshops. It is from you that we have learned so much as you joined in the discussions and activities, offering new, different (and sometimes challenging) perspectives on the parenting journey. We gratefully acknowledge your many contributions. Our workshops (and this book) are richer through your contributions.

To our dear friend, Dr. Anne Fraser, many thanks for poring over the manuscript and crafting an inspiring Foreword.

To our creative photographer, Michael Hewis – you know how to make a picture "sing."

This book would not be possible without Career/LifeSkills Resources for permitting us to use the amazing Personality Dimensions® model. We must thank the facilitation group and principal author Lynda McKim, for developing this temperament model for Career/LifeSkills Resources. Thank you especially for the on-going encouragement, support, editing and direction provided by both Denise Hughes and Brad Whitehorn, whose input has been invaluable as the book unfolded.

Foreword

The book is designed as a parenting **Roadmap**. Whether you see your child as organized like Mary Poppins, a dreamer like Ariel, fun-loving like Peter Pan or inquisitive like Jack Sparrow, this book will thrill and enlighten your imagination and help you see new ways to foster you child's natural inclinations. Great Parenting Skills (GPS) Roadmap helps children explore their positive nature. The Roadmap helps parents to know when to encourage, monitor, recognize and support their child's abilities. It supports the notion that every child has the potential to be "the little engine that could."

The authors Kate and Wayne, take us on an exploratory adventure where the Walt Disney World® Magic Kingdom® Theme Park and its characters emerge with real, usable, meaningful insights into your parenting journey. You will be able to grasp features about your parenting journey that deepen your understanding of your children and yourselves. This is an exciting opportunity to appreciate how relationships with your children develop and are sustained. An important aspect of this book, in my view, is its assimilation of examples from the journals of children. Lived stories are compelling and offer unique personal insight into the complex situations that often cause parental stresses.

Kate and Wayne Jones are parents of two daughters and 4 grandchildren. In their professional lives each is an educator. Kate designs, develops and conducts workshops which focus on experiences for those concerned with the development of our children, primarily parents. Wayne is a retired school principal having spent years navigating various education systems that so deeply affect our students. Whatever affects our children profoundly concerns the adults who care for them. Kate and Wayne have prepared this wonderful, easy-reading, fun-filled and inspiring collection of narratives, lessons and proposals about turning your parenting journey into a "yummy" voyage.

Parents, this book is about two journeys, yours and your child's. You will explore how your respective journeys mesh and how you can better detect the bumps along the way. As you work to smooth out the bumps you may learn to **crack the code** of your child's unique communicating style. Your introverted child will deal with the bumps in a different manner than one who is extroverted.

Great Parenting Skills (GPS) appeal is strengthened by its theoretical, practical and experiential foundations. The book effectively integrates teachings of sages and scholars such as Carl Jung, the Father of Psychology, Dr. Linda Berens, whose works explore the four temperaments, Barbara Coloroso, who describes three kinds of parents and Mary McGuiness, author of *You've got Personality*.

Is your child like a busy beaver, an industrious planner, or maybe your child is a helper, able to create a harmonious atmosphere; or what about the child that is impulsive and changeable or curious, independent and non-conforming? This book will give you the tools to prepare yourselves for your kids' stress signs and suggest some possible antidotes.

I enthusiastically recommend Great Parenting Skills (GPS) to parents, grandparents, teachers, childcare workers and all adults who care deeply for the happiness and growth of children. I believe you will find the book provides enormous reading pleasure and effective practical suggestions to enrich a joyful parenting journey.

Dr. Ruth Anne Fraser, PhD – President
Fraser Education, Uxbridge, Ontario, Canada

Table of Contents

Introduction – "Yummy" or "Yucky"? xiii

Chapter 1 – Ready! Set! Start Your Engines! 1

Chapter 2 – Destination: Disney 15

Chapter 3 – GPS For Your Parenting Journey Preferences 25

Chapter 4 – GPS For Your Children's Journey 37

Chapter 5 – GPS For "Bumps" Along The Way 63

Chapter 6 – GPS For Positive Communication
On Your Journey 93

Chapter 7 – GPS For Introverts & Extraverts
On Your Journey 115

Chapter 8 – GPS For Creating Positive Home
Learning Environments 131

Chapter 9 – Conclusion: The Final GPS
Coordinates Are Yours! 157

Resources 159

Introduction

"Yummy" or "Yucky"?

One Saturday morning we woke up to the smell of coffee and muffins. **Yummm!!!** Our two elementary school-aged daughters flew into our room excited. As they each took one of our arms, they cried in unison, *"Get up! Get up! Breakfast is ready!!"*

The two of us caught one another's eye and smiled as we quickly jumped out of bed. We adored our daughters. We adored Saturday mornings with them. We adored muffins and coffee. What a perfect day!

Wayne couldn't wait to be the first one to bite into one of those delicious-smelling muffins. His eyes watered. His smile vanished. He spit out the muffin. And then he exclaimed, *"Who put all that salt in the muffins?"* **Yuck!!!**

A parent's life is not always positively perfect.

When we told our friends this story you can imagine some of their questions.

"You let them bake?" Yes, the older daughter is usually responsible and capable with the toaster oven.

"Is it their job to cook breakfast?" No. They wanted to do something special for us so we had given them permission to bake muffins that morning.

"Was it your anniversary?" No, not a special day. An ordinary Saturday.

"How much salt did they put in the muffins?" One cup.

"One cup of salt? Isn't that a little much?" Yes; the recipe called for 1 teaspoon of salt.

"So how did they happen to put a whole cup in the mix?" The younger one is excitable and adventurous and we're not too sure whether she read the recipe wrong or was being her creative self, wondering what would happen if she increased the salt content.

"Ah!"

Then the question every one of our friends blurted out, *"What did you do?"* Well, we laughed for quite some time. Then went back to the original recipe and made a yummy batch of muffins that we all enjoyed together. This was a lesson learned by the younger daughter who has, in fact, turned into a fabulous home chef!

That's life with kids! And it is up to you, the parent, whether it is a "yummy" or a "yucky" journey!

The parenting journey can be the "yummiest" journey you will ever take, especially if you have a personal GPS as your guide! Like all journeys, you need a plan, a guide, a map, or a compass to reach your destination. You may not have thought of parenting your children through the growing up years as a "journey." Well, there is a beginning point — when they are born. There is also an end point, a destination: when they reach adulthood and are ready to "take on the world" on their own journey. Moving between those two points in your children's lives is truly a journey. How you move towards that destination is where this book comes into play.

Our mission — the reason we wrote this book — is to provide you with an invaluable tool, a personal GPS, if you will, for your parenting journey. This personal GPS tool will help you understand the innate behavioural patterns of you and your children, so you can turn your parenting journey into a "yummy" experience.

If we can help you experience some of the joy we had guiding our own youngsters through their growing years then we will have accomplished our mission. For us, the joy of going through our parenting journey revolved around discovering the true nature of each of our children. We wanted to know what made them "tick" — what made them happy, what they valued, what stressed them out, what encouraged them, what natural strengths and abilities they possessed, as well as their tendencies towards Introversion or Extraversion.

It was not easy finding the answers to our questions; in fact it was more trial and error with many bumps along the way. We had no consistent roadmap or compass, no personal GPS tool to guide us. This book is your parenting roadmap. We call it your **Great Parenting Skills** (GPS) tool, which we want to share with you to help prevent, or at least alleviate, some of the "yucky" bumps that we encountered on the parenting journey.

By the end of our own parenting journey we had raised two very different people who had, and continued to develop, unique personalities as they moved into their respective adulthood journeys. Through them, we have now entered the grandparenting journey, one that adds yet another layer of understanding people's behaviour. So grandparents — this book is also for you! We often have grandparents attend our workshops. You know the adage, "It's never too late to learn!"

On a professional level, both of us are educators. Can other educators learn about children from this book? Absolutely! After all, the children also attend school and possess the same natures whether at home or at school. As a teacher and administrator his entire career, Wayne learned from the many parents and students with whom he had the opportunity to work. Kate also worked in schools for part of her career and started running workshops for teachers, who then persuaded her to come back and train the parents.

For this book we chose to focus on the parenting journey specifically because so many parents have indicated in our workshops that they would like to have this information at their fingertips. And, for us, it is truly a privilege to provide the information. We certainly acknowledge that every child is unique in their own way. Having said that, we have found that the four distinct patterns of behaviour which will be described in **Chapter One**, have crystallized for us over the years. It is our hope that this book will help you gain a fuller understanding of the four patterns so you can apply this knowledge, and enjoy a "yummy" parenting journey.

Like all journeys, you will no doubt experience bumps and detours. For example, have you sometimes been driving with your vehicular GPS directing you and suddenly the signal is gone? Irritating, huh? Or worse, you may have no idea where to go next. And then the signal pops back on. Phew! Back to using the vehicle's GPS. The same thing happens in your parenting journey. You get a little lost trying to find your way and it can turn "yucky" quickly. Come back to the book and check out your personal GPS to return to a "yummy" parenting journey.

To more fully illustrate the information and add a little fun we have included anecdotes, stories, and little vignettes throughout the journey. Some of them will be our own stories, but most of them are from parents just like you who have shared them with us and are trying to build great family relations, one day at a time!

Great Parenting Skills (GPS)

The "muffin" story could have had a very different ending had we, as parents, not begun to understand the natures of our kids beforehand. For us it had been a "trial and error" experience to figure out what drove each of our children's behaviours. It was only after they both left home that we were introduced to a wonderful tool that provides us with a way to understand people's innate behaviour. As parents, grandparents, and educators, we think it is an invaluable tool to add to your parental toolbox. It is a personal GPS tool that you can follow when you are trying to make sense of their personality style throughout your parenting journey.

If you use this personal GPS tool you will be sure to gain a basic understanding of the natural inclinations of each of your kids. You, in turn, will then be able to guide them into becoming fully functioning adults who contribute positively to their society — in their own way. It is our joy to introduce you to a GPS tool for your parenting journey that will help you and your children reach that goal.

This tool provides you with very specific information about what makes your kids "tick." You will discover that every human being is born to behave in a certain way, including how they communicate, how and why they get stressed, how they learn, and even how they perceive the world. There are four distinct patterns, each very different from the other, which we will describe.

You will be able to use this personal GPS tool to respond lovingly and positively to your children, each of whom were born to act in a specific manner. We will help you see through the lens of your respective children, in other words, to see the world the way they do. You will then gain a greater understanding of your kids, and, in doing so, you can then create an even stronger family unit than you already enjoy.

This book provides the roadmap to help you enjoy your parenting journey. We hope you appreciate the anecdotes from our own lives and from other parents. As two seasoned parents/educators who are now treasuring the journey of the grandparent. And just like you, we continue to learn more about people as we facilitate workshops and listen to your stories.

This personal GPS tool changed our family life forever. We can only hope that it will change yours too. We want to shout it from the housetops — this GPS tool will help you enjoy a "yummy" parenting journey!

What is this Personal GPS Tool?

Did you know that every child is "hard-wired" to behave in a specific way? Often in one family the children are not "hard-wired" to act the same way; that would be too easy for the parent! Think back to when you were growing up. Did you have siblings or perhaps your friends had siblings? Did the siblings behave differently? Our two kids certainly behaved very differently from one another. In fact on occasion, Kate admits that — as a mom — she would sometimes think, "Why can't she be more like her sister?" The irony is that Kate admits she said that about each of our daughters at different times!

Would you like to "crack the code" so you know how your child is hard-wired? The key is as old as Hippocrates! Apparently the ancient Greek physician observed and wrote about four distinct ways that people behaved. Through the centuries since then, experts around the world concur and have provided us with a sophisticated "temperament theory." The theory states that each of us is born with an inherent drive to behave in a specific way, based on specific core needs and values. Now, in the 21st Century, as authors, we have taken the liberty of unofficially referring to it as our personal GPS tool.

The reason we like this theory so much is because it has stood the test of time. Many theories come and go, kind of like the "flavour of the month." We like to say that it is a theory that you can "hang your hat on" knowing that numerous cultures have described four different temperaments, or personality dimensions, throughout the centuries.

If we jump to the opening of the 20th Century we find that Dr. Carl Jung, a Swiss psychologist often thought to be the modern father of personality type theory, wrote *Psychological Types*[1]. Are you one of the many parents that tell us that you have completed something called the MBTI® instrument (Myers-Briggs Type Indicator®)[2]? Did you know that survey was developed by a mother-daughter team (Myers and Briggs) in the mid 20th Century, based on Jung's writing?

Also in the mid-20th Century, Dr. David Keirsey co-authored *Please Understand Me*, and later wrote the sequel, *Please Understand Me II*[3]. Keirsey fully describes the four categories and called them temperaments. Inspired by Keirsey, Don Lowry, a California school teacher, popularized the theory through his *True Colors* survey[4] that he developed in 1979 as an educational, interactive model for students. Perhaps you have also completed this survey, which spread like wildfire throughout schools and businesses in the late 80's and 90's?

In this century, Dr. Linda Berens has continued to study and write about the four temperaments in her book *Understanding Yourself and Others: An Introduction to the 4 Temperaments, 4.0*[5], along with others we'll introduce throughout this book. In 2003 Career/ LifeSkills Resources Inc. introduced *Personality Dimensions*® (PD)[6] as a representation of the next level of development in refining temperament, or personality dimension, theory. We are delighted to use Personality Dimensions® as our vehicle for our personal GPS tool for parents since, first of all, it is based on the latest research, and secondly, PD was developed by Canadians and we are both proud Canadians! In this book we will be using the four temperament, or dimension, terms as described in the tool *Personality Dimensions*®, namely: Organized Gold, Authentic Blue, Resourceful Orange and Inquiring Green.

Why Invest Your Valuable Time in this GPS?

This is a short-term investment for life-long results. No kidding! For over a decade now we have used this personality dimension theory almost daily! Wayne, an educator for over four decades, may want to tell me a funny story or an interesting anecdote about a student and all he has to say is something like, *"This student is very likely an Inquiring Green."* That sets the scene so I have a more complete understanding of the situation he is about to describe.

Another way of looking at this book as time well spent is that you may find yourself saying as a parent about your child *"If I were you, I'd do........."* Once you spend a little time learning this GPS you may find yourself saying something like, *"I know how much you like ...; so you might want to try......."* See the difference? It is so much more positive and helpful!

By spending some valuable time learning this **GPS** tool, you will:

- better understand yourself
- better understand other adults who play a role in your kid's life
- better understand your children
- appreciate your kid's particular set of strengths
- appreciate that your offspring may be very different from you
- allow your children to develop their own tendencies and strengths
- understand stresses specific to your nature and that of your kids
- appreciate the differences in, and at the same time adapt to different situations
- connect with your kids in a more positive manner (well, most of the time anyway)
- build a stronger foundation of trust, acknowledgement and positivity with each of your kids, no matter how different they may be from you
- enjoy strong family ties that will continue into their adulthood

Chapter 1

READY! SET! START YOUR ENGINES!

You are now ready for a test run of Personality Dimensions® theory, or your personal GPS, as we will refer to it from now on! It is time for you to get a better understanding of your own profile before looking at the way your kids behave. For all you *Harry Potter* fans, this is akin to the "Sorting Ceremony" where the first year students at Hogwarts School of Witchcraft and Wizardry were placed in one of four houses according to their nature. The difference is you get to choose the answers here, based on what makes you feel good, or what you feel is your natural inclination. The following ten questions are not about what you can do, or even what you should do, but what you would choose in each of the questions. And the great thing about this little quiz — there are no wrong answers! So don't sweat it! Just have fun selecting the way you like!

Complete the next **ten** questions by rating the four statements. Give the phrase a number 4 if it reflects you the best, 3 if it is a lot like you, 2 if it is a little like you, and 1 if it is least like you. Each phrase must get a different number. Got that?

So the highest rating is a 4 and the lowest rating is a 1.

 4 = most like you
 3 = almost like you
 2 = a little like you
 1 = least like you

1. I am at my happiest when I...

A.	_____	Find meaning in life
B.	_____	Feel included by others
C.	_____	Have mastered knowledge and competence
D.	_____	Feel free to do what I want

2. I am skilled at...

A.	_____	Counselling / Coaching / Mentoring
B.	_____	Planning
C.	_____	Analyzing
D.	_____	Trouble shooting

3. I would describe my communication style as...

A.	_____	Very Expressive, Convincing, Motivational
B.	_____	Clear, Precise, Detailed
C.	_____	Objective, Directed, Pointed
D.	_____	Charismatic, Enthusiastic, Persuasive

4. At work I am...

A.	_____	Supportive, Enthusiastic, Flexible
B.	_____	Organized, Committed, Dependable
C.	_____	Competent, Innovative, Enquiring
D.	_____	Energetic, Entrepreneurial, Realistic

5. In relationships I look for...

A.	_____	Connections, Intimacy, Meaning
B.	_____	Loyalty, Commitment, Honesty
C.	_____	Directness, Honour, Mental Stimulation
D.	_____	Spontaneity, Commonality, Excitement

6. I become stressed when there is...

A.	_____	Conflict, Criticism, Lack of Feeling
B.	_____	Disorder, Instability, Procrastination
C.	_____	Incompetence, Injustice, Sentimentality
D.	_____	Rules, Authority, No Action

7. I am encouraged by...

A.	_____	Emotional Support, Personal Validation
B.	_____	Recognition of contribution
C.	_____	Recognition of intelligence
D.	_____	Applause, Respect, Admiration

8. I would describe my favourite learning environment as one that is...

A.	_____	Cooperative, Safe, Conceptual
B.	_____	Structured, Specific, Practical
C.	_____	Independent, Analytical, Rational
D.	_____	Skill-based, Applied, Varied

9. I am interested in...

A.	_____	People development
B.	_____	Data that supports people and organizations
C.	_____	Concepts and ideas
D.	_____	Actions that have an impact

10. In groups, I tend to be...

A.	_____	Cooperative, Inspirational, Communicative
B.	_____	Organized, Committed, Responsible
C.	_____	Independent, Analytical, Strategic
D.	_____	Energetic, Creative, Fun

To Score:

For each question, transcribe the numbers you allocated for each of A, B, C, D on the next page.

Add the scores for each of the columns.

Record the totals for each of the columns.

Example

Question	A	B	C	D
# 1	4	2	1	3
/\				
Total	27	12	19	4

Question	A	B	C	D
# 1				
# 2				
# 3				
# 4				
# 5				
# 6				
# 7				
# 8				
# 9				
# 10				
Total				

If your highest score is A you are primarily an Authentic Blue.

If your highest score is B you are primarily an Organized Gold.

If your highest score is C you are primarily an Inquiring Green.

If your highest score is D you are primarily a Resourceful Orange.

Did you enjoy the test run? We hope so!

In the evening of the day that Kate completed her PD course we happened to have a family dinner party. Our very enthusiastic, fun-loving daughter (then a young adult) who was always ready for something new and exciting insisted that we all take the quiz immediately. As Kate watched the reactions of each family member to this suggestion she was struck at how true to character the individual's reaction was that night. At that moment she understood how invaluable a tool this is to a family.

We Are All a Blend!

Did you also notice that you likely didn't answer all of the questions as an A, a B, a C, or a D? Your highest score is most likely your preferred style, your lowest score would be your least preferred style, etc. So now you can fill in the chart below to know what your "colour profile" is, based on this simple test.

My Hightest Preference	My 2nd Preference	My 3rd Preference	My Lowest Preference

This is your personal blend of all of the dimensions. So while you likely lean towards one pattern of behaviour you can and do function from all the patterns to a greater or lesser degree. People, after all, are very complicated! We also can and do adapt our natural leanings as required throughout our stages of life. As parents, we don't use this theory to "pigeon hole" our children, but to better understand their natural inclinations so that we in turn can adapt to them. That's the cool part; we can adapt our own behaviour to our children's so we can better parent them! But more of that later.

Introvert or Extravert? Another Dimension to GPS

While we talk about four personality patterns that are easy to understand, *Personality Dimensions®* also includes Introversion/ Extraversion as a vital part of human behaviour in temperament theory. This is one more reason we chose *Personality Dimensions®* as our particular vehicle for our *GPS for Navigating Your Kid's Personality!*

We consider the whole discussion of Introversion and Extraversion to be so vital to understanding people that we have written an entire chapter on it. So, if you are someone who cannot wait for **Chapter 7**, skip to it now for more details and a fun questionnaire to discover whether you are an "inny" or an "outy!"[7]

Your Roadmap for Your Parenting Journey

Here's a roadmap for the rest of this book. You can choose to follow the map methodically, or jump around on your journey. It's up to you! Just have fun as you learn more about yourself and your children!

Chapter 2: *Destination: Disney*
This chapter will describe the core needs and values of each of the innate natures, with a little help from Walt Disney World® Magic Kingdom® Theme Park.

Chapter 3: *GPS for Your Parenting Journey Preferences*
In this chapter you will explore the parenting preferences according to the four dimensions. You will also discover whether your personality corresponds to your parenting preference.

Chapter 4: *GPS for Your Children's Journey Preferences*
This chapter will be a discovery of your children's innate skills, abilities and ways to encourage them to confidently develop these natural attributes. We hope you enjoy the vignettes we have included!

Chapter 5: *GPS for Bumps Along The Way*
In this chapter, you will find out what stresses each of the dimensions and how you can alleviate this concern.

Chapter 6: *GPS for Positive Communication On Your Journey*
In this chapter you will discover the communication styles of each personality dimension. With a little help from some Disney characters we hope you will enjoy great conversations with your kids while on your journey.

Chapter 7: *GPS for Introverts and Extraverts On Your Journey*
This chapter provides you with insight into what is often the easiest difference to spot, yet the one facet least understood: Introversion and Extraversion (I/E). We take you on four road trips to introduce you to the I/E component for each dimension, supplemented by examples of two Disney characters for each combination.

Chapter 8: *GPS for Creating Positive Home Learning Environments*
This chapter brings you back home to where you will learn how to create the best learning environment for your children's innate personality dimension. It is our hope that armed with this knowledge you can put a stop — or at least slow down — some of the homework wars you tell us about!

So that is the whole journey in a nutshell! You now have an idea of where we are taking you. You also have an idea of your own natural leanings and of your blend. You may be wondering "so what?" How does this help me as a person, or as a parent, to build better relations and create a tighter family unit? Let's have some fun and go on a quick trip to Walt Disney World® to begin our journey of discovery.

Chapter 2

DESTINATION: DISNEY

"We're going to Disney!!!" Squeals of delight — dancing — jumping up and down! More squeals of delight. That was the scene in our living room when we announced to our young daughters that we were driving to Florida on March break and spending three days in the Walt Disney World® Magic Kingdom® Theme Park! That same scene was repeated a number of years later when we made the same announcement to our grandchildren!

Everyone knows that Walt Disney dreamed up one of the most magical places on earth for children of all ages. But did you know that part of its magic is the way he initially divided it into four distinct magical lands?" And furthermore, did you know that each of his magical lands provides us with a wonderful way to look at the four innate natures? It was Stephen Montgomery[1] who introduced us to this notion that Disney's magical lands are a fun way of understanding the natural inclinations of our own little "characters" — our kids!

If you were to ask yourself, "What do I want for my child/children?" most people would answer something like, "I just want my kids to do well and be happy." With the Positive Psychology field blooming profusely there is a lot being studied and written about being happy and what it truly means to be happy. In his book, *Authentic Happiness*, Dr. Martin Seligman, former president of the American Psychological Association, explains that Positive Psychology is more than 'happiology' or those hedonistic, fleeting moments. You know the kind of happiness you get when you eat a heavenly, decadent dessert or win a soccer match or buy that favourite pair of jeans you have been wanting. Dr. Seligman explains that Positive Psychology is about achieving "authentic happiness."[2] "Authentic happiness" is about understanding our own well-being by first of all understanding our personal strengths and virtues, and then using these strengths and virtues daily to carve out a meaningful life. The result? We feel good; we feel happy, if you will. You can help your children achieve authentic happiness as you put it into practice yourself on the parenting journey.

Did you know there is a Happiness Line? Psychologist/researcher Michael Fordyce demonstrated "that happiness can be statistically measured."[3] The Fordyce Emotions Survey[4] is a graphic organizer that gives us an overview of a range of emotions, on a scale from 1 (extremely unhappy: utterly depressed, completely down) to 10 (extremely happy: feeling ecstatic, joyous, fantastic). It is an important breakthrough that tells you as parents that having a positive outlook and increasing your happiness is a possibility, for you and for your children.

What does authentic happiness have to do with *GPS for Navigating Your Kids Personality?* Part of the "roadmap" includes knowing that at the core of each personality dimension there is a need specific to that group of people[5]. If that need is met how do you think each group of people feels? In *Spontaneous Happiness*, Dr. Andrew Weill states that "many people seek happiness 'out there,'"[6] but happiness is really about creating "an internal state of well-being."[7] We believe that if parents strive to understand and embrace the **core need** of their children, then those children have a better chance of being closer to the top of the happiness line more often. You want your kids to **feel good**, and think life is good.

As a parent, it may be easier to figure out which personality dimension your child falls in by noticing what they value, or what they find virtuous. What they perceive is important, including principles to live by, a specific code of behaviour, what they yearn for, what they put their trust in, even what they prize or what they aspire towards. We like to think of it in terms of *what makes your kids feel like they have had a successful day?* If their **values** have been recognized as important by others then they feel they have accomplished something good. They **feel successful**, or think of themselves as being successful.

So let's have some fun learning more about this personal GPS and journey to the four original lands of Disney to peek into the marvelous world of each of the four basic natures. For it is here that you will begin to understand GPS for yourself. As we stroll through the Walt Disney World® Magic Kingdom® Theme Park, you will see what makes each of the four dimensions experience authentic happiness when their core need is met; they **feel good**, and by embracing their values, they **feel successful**.

Main Street, U.S.A.® and Organized Golds

Once Organized Gold children pass the gates and walk through the tunnel under the Walt Disney World® Railroad they immediately feel a sense of **belonging** for they are standing in the Town Square of Main Street U.S.A.®8. They recognize the organized pattern of the Town Square that includes a City Hall, a Barber Shop and a restaurant, just as they would in any small town, where everyone has specific **duties** and **responsibilities**. But wait — Disney has turned back the clock to depict a small town at the turn of the 20th Century. Organized Golds feel an overwhelming sense of security steeped in the historical, and perhaps safer, past. Their excitement rises as they realize they can enjoy a ride in a horseless carriage, an homage to their penchant for tradition. They feel comforted by the fact that some things never change on a Main Street; there will always be hometown staples like a cinema, a bakery, an ice-cream parlour and a candy store.

What Makes Organized Golds Feel Good?

If Organized Gold kids feel like they **belong** to the community in which they live, work and play then they feel good; they may well give life a "high five" on the Happiness Line!

Organized Gold children will actively enhance their need of belonging by taking on **duties** and **responsibilities**, even at a young age. It is their way of feeling that they belong in their family. How does this translate in real life? As a child, one of Wayne's duties included putting up the lights outside during the holidays. He started by helping his dad with the lights and eventually, proudly, took it on as his own task until he left home. As Organized Golds grow they often express their sense of worth through belonging to the family by taking on more age-appropriate responsibilities. They may start out helping you set the table, collect the wash, to eventually driving their younger siblings to practices, or running errands for you.

What Makes Organized Golds Feel Successful?

Organized Golds seek **security**. Security translates into having an organized system for everything. The Boy Scout motto, "Be Prepared" is reflected in what is pretty much a way of life for Organized Gold kids.

These children also have "plan B" right through to a "plan Z" if they feel it is necessary to maintain a secure life. This is the reason that they put so much trust in **tradition**; they can look back at how things have worked in the past and feel secure that things will work out as planned. For example, if you always picked them up in time for piano lessons after school last year they trust that you will get them to martial arts class on time this year. However, they also want to know what to do, for example, if you don't pick them up at the appointed time. One mom tells us that when her young Organized Gold gets off the school bus she knows if mom is not there to not panic, but go into the local school and call her mom's cell number, which she carries in her backpack. Older children will likely have their own cell phone with all emergency numbers listed on the phone's contact list.

For Organized Golds rules **rock**! Rules make the world go round in their world. Think of the security that rules bring to Organized Golds. Rules provide a way of doing a job that tradition has shown works. For example, for Organized Gold kids that might mean if they go to bed at the same time every night, they will get enough sleep so they can wake up at the correct time in the morning to get on with the day as planned, starting with having time for breakfast and getting ready. Did you catch the **detailed steps** in that example?

Organized Golds don't just want the rules, they ask for them from you, the **authority** figure in their lives because, as is their nature, they inherently respect you. And more often than not they want to follow the exact steps to create **predictable routines**. Organized Golds want to know how they are going to get their piano practice done, their homework completed, and still have screen time every evening after school.

It follows that if they have planned carefully, the Organized Golds will **finish what they started**, which is something they value. They want to know there is a beginning, a middle, and an end to things. This is a goal-oriented dimension that works towards completing the task. One parent told us that her child signed up for a running program at school. To run the 5-kilometre race in the late spring her child needed to follow an organized plan every week. Her child looked forward to finishing the race in a specific amount of time so started practicing earlier in the year than many of the other kids. She proudly announced that her child not only finished the race, but with a better time than previous practice runs!

Organized Golds are **concerned** citizens of the world. These kids start at a very young age to be concerned about the little things in life, like getting their chores done as requested. They will show concern for siblings and get to events/programs on time. As they grow up they become concerned about the bigger things in life, such as their classmates, their neighbourhood, their friends, and society standards.

You may now be able to begin to appreciate the reasons that your Organized Gold children are particularly happy and attracted to the organized stability of Main Street U.S.A.®. The area depicts a small town with traditional, secure establishments where the shopkeepers attend to daily tasks as they welcome the whole family and provide a sense of community.

Fantasyland® and Authentic Blues

When Authentic Blue kids walk through *Cinderella's Castle* at Walt Disney World® Magic Kingdom® Theme Park they enter *Fantasyland®*. It is a land separated from all other lands; a place where these imaginative children can believe that anything is possible. They can dream of idealistic **relationships** through romantic fairy tales that come to life here, such as *Peter Pan's Flight®*. They can now enjoy an interactive story adventure at the *Enchanted Tales with Belle®*. When riding *"it's a small world®"*, they love seeing the people represented by the many cultures, even as they will continue to pursue their own identity, their personal meaning, to **become better people**. They will always want the whole world to be as happy as *"it's a small world®"* depicts. While eating at *Pinocchio Village Haus* they too wish to become as authentic and honest as Pinocchio did to achieve **harmony** in all of their relationships.

What Makes Authentic Blues Feel Good?

Authentic Blues yearn for deep interpersonal **relationships** with the people who surround them. They would give their lives a high number on the *Happiness Line* when all of their relationships are good.

To experience deep interpersonal relations Authentic Blues seek **harmony** within the family, while at the same time working to become the **best person** they can be so they earn the title of being authentic. How might this play out in real life? These children often look for the positive in others while also looking at the uniqueness of each individual. We have heard many stories about Authentic Blue children acting as the mediator between two or three feuding friends on the playground or with siblings. One such child lamented to her parent that she just didn't see "why people can't simply get along!"

What Makes Authentic Blues Feel Successful?

Authentic Blues can be highly emotional people who often openly express their emotions in a warm, friendly, positive way. They often express their emotions and beliefs with limitless enthusiasm. Authentic Blue children will eagerly discuss their ideas or their personal insights in such a way that you catch their **enthusiasm**. They may even inspire you to give to a needy charity, or to volunteer with them in a soup kitchen.

Even at a young age Authentic Blues begin to trust their **intuition**, their feelings and first impressions about others. It might very well be due to the fact that they possess an ability to identify with others and want to "walk in the other person's shoes." They may see patterns and leap to conclusions that other personality dimensions won't or can't do. For example, our intuitive Authentic Blue toddler would sense if mommy was having a bad day by asking, "What's wrong mommy?" That same toddler grew up to become an art therapist.

Authentic Blues are **romantic idealists** who desire deep, meaningful relationships and value **being with others**. Young Authentic Blues wait for the storyline, "and they lived happily ever after," wanting to believe that this is true for all people, especially those closest to them. They value deep relationships with family members and friends. They want to always be able to share their deepest selves with those around them. From a very young age these kids want best friends, and often have imaginary friends for quite some time. Our own very Blue granddaughter had one whom she called "Monster" for some reason; Monster was of the good variety!

Authentic Blues really don't get caught up in **details**. In fact they don't want to be bothered with the small details in life. They tend to get the full picture or the overview and feel that is enough. It is as though they want to see the forest, not all of the trees within the forest. One Authentic Blue child lamented to her parents that she could not understand, for example, why she had to show all of the steps in an equation in her math exams, since she could jump over some steps and still get the right answer!

Achieving **approval from others** is highly valued by Authentic Blue children. To some extent this may appear to be a good thing for parents. However, if these children continue to constantly want approval and so strive to please everyone, it can get exhausting for them, not to mention unhealthy. However, having said that, it is part of their value system, and it does tend to help them find a harmonious balance in their relationships with others.

Authentic Blues often grow up to become the "helpers" in the world, such as therapists, motivational speakers, psychologists and elementary school teachers. They often spend their lives encouraging others and so, as youngsters, appreciate **encouragement** from you. One grandparent disclosed that he often would tell his Authentic Blue grandson that it was ok to do something, such as go weed the garden, or feed the grandparents' dog, or go next door to play with the neighbour's children.

Paying **attention** to your Authentic Blue is vitally important to these children. When you think about it they want to please you, so may do chores around the house, take care of siblings, make peace, all without being asked to do so. But they do want you to realize that they have done all of this. As one Authentic Blue adult told us, "I just want a little thanks and I'm happy to continue doing what I have been doing all of my life!" Another parent said that sometimes she has to simply smile at her eldest child who is an Authentic Blue when she does something nice for her younger sibling, such as reaching for a cup that is too high for the little one.

Hopefully you now have gained an understanding for the reasons your Authentic Blues are specifically happy and drawn to the harmonious Fantasyland®. Here they enjoy watching imaginary characters building the kinds of good relationships they dream of for themselves. It is a land of "happily ever after" for the "good" people who become even better, and where the "bad" people are "banished" in one way or another.

Adventureland® and Resourceful Oranges

Resourceful Orange kids walk (or usually run) from Main Street U.S.A.® over a wooden plank bridge to get to their favourite area, *Adventureland®*. For these **freedom**-seeking children the theme in **Adventureland®** seems to be "anything goes!" Not only are there lots of **activities** to keep these busy children happy but variety abounds too. For example, they can climb the *Swiss Family Treehouse*, fly over a desert in T*he Magic Carpets of Aladdin®*, explore the jungle on *Jungle Cruise®*, or on the adventurous high seas with Jack Sparrow, the notorious pirate, on the *Pirates of the Caribbean®* ride, or — well, you get it. So many things to keep them actively entertained. Whew!

What Makes Resourceful Oranges Feel Good?

Resourceful Oranges yearn for **freedom** — a lack of restrictions. They don't want to be micromanaged or feel constrained in anything, or by anyone, including their parents, grandparents, and/or teachers. They are near the top of the happy line when they gain freedom of choice in what they do, in making decisions, and in expressing themselves.

Resourceful Orange children will constantly look for **variety** within all the possible **activities** that will give them the freedom they desire. For example, they might move from painting a picture, to playing an instrument, to jumping on a trampoline — all in a matter of minutes. When there isn't any action they will quickly tell you how bored they are and expect you to come up with something new and fun to occupy them. The good news is that it doesn't take a whole lot to engage these children. Wayne tells the story of a snowy February when the students had to stay in for recess every day for a very long week. He watched a Resourceful Orange grade 2 student hopping down the hallway using the pattern on the floor as a long hop scotch trail, smiling all the way! Students were supposed to walk down the hallways but this one clearly found that a little boring so made it much more fun.

What Makes Resourceful Oranges Feel Successful?

Resourceful Oranges don't just enjoy being **excited**, but insist upon it, especially if they are a little bored with life. Their motto would be something like, "never a dull moment!" Living with Resourceful Oranges means action, adventure, restless energy, thrills, spills, and even calculated risks. Theirs is a "delicious" excitement for life that continues into adulthood.

Part of their excitement in life depends on the **freedom to decide quickly**; a spontaneous aliveness that Resourceful Oranges value. "Just do it" is something you'll often hear them say. Since they live for the moment Resourceful Oranges, especially children, usually trust their impulses. As children, this often means acting without thinking things through. For this personality dimension that is the ultimate freedom. In our experience, this child grows up having to say "sorry" more often than not for their somewhat impulsive actions! They learn from consistent boundaries, but rigid rules may just spark rebellion.

Resourceful Oranges are frequently the first ones to **try something new**. They may try new dives at the pool before their peers will, or be the first to do a fancy manoeuvre on the skateboard or snowboard. When we dropped into *Disney's Pop Century Resort* and saw a huge replica of a Big Wheel, we stopped and commented on its appeal for the very active Resourceful Oranges. Just at that moment, a young dad remarked to us excitedly how he had so enjoyed doing all kinds of tricks on his Big Wheel, and then went on to tell us of some of his misadventures growing up and trying every new, crazy thing he could think of to do with bikes. Hmmm... think he might be a Resourceful Orange?

Resourceful Oranges value making an impact on their society, and **having their skills noticed**. They want to make their mark, so to speak. They want you to notice what they can do. Hand-in-hand with this need to have their skills noticed is the value they place on having a **chance to perform**. They want you to watch and appreciate their playing/singing a solo musical piece, or scoring a touchdown, or writing a really good article. As the parent of one Resourceful Orange told Kate, "They may only have an audience of one, and that one can be you, the parent!"

Resourceful Oranges value **being in control** of their lives. For the most part, they don't want to control anybody else, just themselves. Providing them with a little leeway to do so will go a long way toward having children who are happy and positive to be around. How can you do that with youngsters? Sometimes it is just a matter of giving them two or three choices, so they feel as though they are in control. For example, you will have a bedtime hour, which will get later as they grow into teen years, but you may give your young Resourceful Orange a choice of doing two or three different things before bed. Given the freedom to choose between these activities gives them a feeling of being in control.

They also like to **work with little supervision**. We know that can be scary for parents to hear. If you try it in some small ways initially, they will understand the trust you are placing in them. As they grow into teenagers they will appreciate the trust you have shown them all along and live up to that trust, for the most part. When she was sixteen, our Resourceful Orange daughter wanted to go to Africa to help build a school in a small village. She had to earn $4,000 to make the trip. We knew that she could do it without too much supervision because we had started in small ways giving her jobs to do without micromanaging her. By her teen years she knew she would only be allowed to work with little supervision if she got the job done. She did earn the money to go to Africa.

Resourceful Oranges want to have the **freedom to create**, or, in other words, they want to be able to do away with the rules so they can be resourceful! They may follow the adage, "better to ask for forgiveness later, than ask for permission first!" They can take what they have and create something out of it. It reminds us of Andy Warhol who looked at a simple can of Campbell's soup and created *Campbell's Soup Cans*[9], consisting of 32 canvases, one for each of the varieties of Campbell's soup available at the time. In 1962 Warhol displayed his work in a one-man exhibition, which marked the West Coast debut of pop art!

We hope you have caught your breath in time to understand why your Resourceful Oranges enjoy Adventureland®. These little adventurers love having the freedom to move from one activity to the next in short order, if you let them! And the variety here far exceeds anything in the other lands, which is what they seek in their own lives!

Tomorrowland® and Inquiring Greens

For the **knowledge**-thirsty Inquiring Greens, *Tomorrowland®*
provides them with **intellectual freedom** to explore the world of
science and technology in a fun way. There is a "sci-fi" atmosphere
in *Tomorrowland®* that appeals to these kids who are drawn to the
notion of **achievement** from a very young age. The neon, glass
and gleaming metal used throughout this part of Walt Disney World®
Magic Kingdom® Theme Park have a futuristic feel that makes the
Inquiring Green want to explore every inch. For example, *Space
Mountain®*, a large dome that houses a roller coaster that blasts kids
into blackness, lit only by stars accompanied by the sound of fleeting
asteroids and other space objects. These children who love to see
"the big picture" can't wait to get on the *Astro Orbiter®* that takes them
revolving above the Magic Kingdom® Theme Park in a rocket allowing
them to see the entire Kingdom. Our Inquiring Green grandson
frequently talks about emission-free cars, so it was no surprise when
we visited *Tomorrowland®* with him that he requested that we all ride
the *Tomorrowland Transit Authority People Mover®* — an innovative
emission-free mass transit system. Another ride we shared with him
was the *Walt Disney Carousel of Progress* where you travel through
the 20th century to see how technology improved living conditions.
He had a few questions for us afterward, especially around the fact
that our grandparents could attest to all of the changes depicted in
this ride, since they were around at the beginning of the last century.

What Makes Inquiring Greens Feel Good?

Inquiring Greens yearn for **knowledge**. It is as though they are on a
quest for the rest of their lives to know and understand. A "high five"
for them on the happiness line is when they discover a new fact,
new data. It's as though they are always looking for that moment
when they can say "Eureka!"

They seek an **intellectual freedom** that allows them to discover for themselves why things work the way they do in whatever system they find fascinating: mechanical, organic or social. This becomes their mission in life with little interest in the daily routines that they may view as a waste of their time. The good news is that they will respect you as their authority figure if you can help them move towards feeling competent in mastering knowledge. For example, when our grandson was five years old, Kate borrowed his dad's tripod for her camera. Not knowing how the camera fit on, she asked her grandson to show her; he certainly demonstrated being high on the happy line that moment as this kindergartener demonstrated his technical "know how" with pride.

What Makes Inquiring Greens Feel Successful?

Inquiring Greens value **theoretical concepts**, or simply put, finding new ways of looking at the world. They ask questions that start with "What if?" and then proceed to brainstorm all kinds of answers — some very "far-fetched" — some people would argue. For them this is fun because theories and concepts fascinate them. For the activity, "Where would you choose to go for a Holiday?" in one of our workshop sessions, a group of Inquiring Greens fantasized going to Mars to explore the unexplored!

Inquiring Greens ask questions that revolve around **progress and improvement**. They prefer to look ahead at "what could be" rather than looking back at "what was." They rely on their knowledge base to ask the right questions that will lead to futuristic answers. According to one parent, some years ago their young teen adamantly suggested that society must change our gas-guzzling cars to a far more efficient method. He outlined a strategy of electrically-run vehicles with power stations every so many kilometres, etc. We are now seeing power plug-ins in many designated areas.

Inquiring Greens value the **freedom to ask "why?"** As you can see from the above example, this question leads to progress. At a young age, though, their "why?" may be about anything because they are just beginning to figure out what interests them. Sometimes they ask questions that we have never bothered to think about because it was not important to us. It is important to them to find out, to explore, and to ask the questions that lead to answers. One parent noticed that her Inquiring Green was constantly asking things about the human body that she simply did not know. "I was not a nurse or a doctor, and I had never thought about how our eyes see, for example," she told us. Fortunately for this mother, there are many books on the human body, some of which are written for very young, inquisitive children!

Inquiring Greens value **intelligence**, both in themselves and in others. They like to think things through rather than having an authority figure (that is you or their teachers) tell them what to think, when to think, or how to think. For that reason they want to make their own decisions about pretty much everything. It allows them to use their knowledge and that, in turn, drives them to expand on that knowledge. As an example, they will often push themselves to move from one level of a game to the next level, and the next, to test and expand on their knowledge.

The interesting thing about Inquiring Greens is the **high standards** that they set for themselves, along with the high standards to which they hold you. You may see this in a young child who wants to put their own clothes on, with no help, including doing up the buttons and the laces at a very young age. In some of the high school science fairs you will see projects by Inquiring Greens who have clearly set very high standards for themselves. Kate attended high school with a couple of Inquiring Greens who were never satisfied until they had solved the most difficult math questions in the text, usually without the teacher's help. These two went on to enter engineering programs at a university on scholarships!

In order to use their intelligence and achieve their own high standards, the Inquiring Green values **independence**. They often don't wish to be in groups, or hang out with friends frequently. They want to be able to explore, to read, to research in their own way. They just want to get on with it on their own. In fact, they live by their own laws and question any rules or regulations that they don't see as necessary. They will independently analyze others' rules and decide for themselves what is right or wrong just as they analyze ideas and decide for themselves whether their ideas are good or bad.

Along with their independence, they value **thinking time**. You may find that they are sitting "looking into space," as one parent described it. They are generally thinking about how something works, and probably formulating their next "why?" question. In fact, they lose track of time as they think through projects. As a result they can be quite oblivious to the fact that it is dinner time, or time to walk the dog, or time to get their other homework done. They sometimes just get caught up in their own thinking space.

As you can now imagine, while Inquiring Greens enjoy friends and family and may have a wide social network, they also want independence and thinking time and value their privacy. This then provides opportunity to explore concepts, ideas, and notions without interruption. You will often see Inquiring Greens in a little corner by themselves reading, working on a laptop, playing with a device; carving out privacy the best way they can.

Now we hope you can understand the reasons your Inquiring Greens are drawn to *Tomorrowland*®. It is a place where these curious kids can freely explore some of the intellectual achievements of the world. They can experience some of the progress made in the past century with an eye to the futuristic possibilities in their lifetime!

You have "scratched the surface" of gaining a good understanding of GPS that will go a long way to bringing true joy into the lives of your children as you continue your parenting journey. You now have more insight into the core needs and values of the "characters" that live under your roof, and there is still a lot more to learn on this journey. For now, let's turn the lens on you, the parents, in our next chapter.

Chapter 3

GPS FOR YOUR PARENTING JOURNEY

On your parenting journey, you may read books. You may start watching (and often judging) how your friends are parenting. You may think back to your own parents and how they parented you (again with the judging). You may Google all kinds of topics on parenting. You may start asking questions of everyone, from your doctor, to your friends, to your co-workers. And the reason for all of this activity, often before the newborn even arrives, is that you want to be the "perfect" parent, better than anyone you know, so that, ultimately, your children will be happy.

You may not realize that you have already formed some real personality style preferences for your parenting role, as did anyone else who may have a hand at raising your kids! However, once your children were born, it likely didn't take you long to realize that just as there are differences in personalities there are differences in parenting preferences!

Just to be clear, we are not talking about what kind of parent you are necessarily. Briefly, here is how Barbara Coloroso[1] describes three kinds of parents, all of which you will find in all four personality dimensions. They include the demanding "Brickwall" parent ('do as I say or else'), the over-indulgent "Jellyfish" parent ('whatever you like is fine by me') or the balanced "Backbone" parent ('has control but is not controlling').

We are talking about the personality style you bring to your parenting role. In **Chapter 1** you have already discovered what personality type fits you in general. You have been introduced to the personality type of your children in **Chapter 2**. The next part of the road map in your GPS is to understand and explore your parenting personality. Is it different than your personality type in general? In some cases it is; in other cases it is the same.

See if you can figure out your preference in the parenting role from the descriptions below. We have included the animal icon suggested by David Keirsey[2] for each dimension to give you a quick idea of what you might look like. We also use Mary McGuiness'[3] one-word description of each type to help you figure out which is your preferred way of parenting. When Kate first created her workshops for parents she gleaned some of the temperament information from both Keirsey[4] and Montgomery[5]. However, now, for *GPS for Navigating Your Kid's Personality*, much of the information is what we have gathered from years of input from parents like you, and we have included our choice of a one-word description of each parenting type.

Are You on the Organized Gold Parenting Journey?

If Organized Gold is your parenting preference the animal that represents your parenting style is the **beaver**. Just like the beaver, you create a detailed plan for getting jobs done. And then you set off to complete it, working methodically and efficiently to do so in a specified amount of time. Think of the beaver meticulously constructing its home in the middle of a pond.

Your motto would be that of the Boy Scout: "**Be Prepared!**" That means you have a schedule of events for your entire family — probably with a big calendar posted on the wall somewhere in your house, often the kitchen. You want to know where everyone is at all times. You likely have that same calendar linked to all of your devices. You also have everyone's contact information at your fingertips so if there is a change in plans you can immediately respond.

Like the beaver, you prefer to lead an **orderly** life — "a place for everything and everything in its place." That applies to your children, as well as all of the paraphernalia that comes with them! Kate remembers that her own father (whose parenting preference was Organized Gold) had a workbench where each and every tool had its specified place. He just had to walk into the area and would know immediately if one of his kids had "borrowed" a tool without returning it to its proper place. Dad would call out something like, *"who has my hammer?"* and one of his kids would scuttle off to retrieve it. He allowed them to use the tools (when age appropriate) but those tools had to be returned to their rightful places, ready for the next project!

Did you catch the other trait from Kate's dad's example? Not only are they orderly but Organized Gold parents are the voice of authority, saying "**follow my rules**." If your parenting preference is Organized Gold then you have created rules for most occasions, from bed time to curfew hour, to screen time, to ... well you get the idea. And you have very likely made it clear to your children that these rules should be followed to maintain order within the family unit.

Mary McGuiness refers to Organized Golds as the **Investigators**. We like the word **Detective** for those who have this parenting style. You like to maintain the family institution and if things are not in order you will investigate immediately. Your kids know that if they don't follow the rules their detective parent will get to the bottom of it, whether it means meeting with their teacher, friends' parents, or even their friends, for answers.

As for discipline, parents who assume an Organized Gold parenting preference traditionally believe that their children must be taught to follow the rules and if they break the rules there should be consequences. It is for the children's good so they will grow up to be model citizens. Some may even call this form of parenting a little **strict**; if you choose this method of parenting you would likely say it is the way you demonstrate your love. These parents will dutifully sacrifice their own needs to meet those of their children, believing it is the responsible thing to do.

In summary, parents who choose the Organized Golds' parenting preference usually assume the role of **family caretaker**. As one parent told us, "I want to ensure that my children are ready to face the world, prepared for everything that may challenge them." They believe that this is the true road to happiness for children. Their kids will be given a plan, and, if they choose to execute it, will be able to follow the plan in an orderly fashion, doing what is right throughout their lives. Their kids will have learned how to follow the rules of society to become responsible citizens who give back. These parents believe they are the primary authorities in their children's lives and will parent accordingly.

Are You on the Authentic Blue Parenting Journey?

If this is your parenting style you are represented by the **dolphin**, which, as we all know, like to swim together in pods and communicate with other dolphins constantly. Like the dolphin you want to be connected with your family members as much as possible. You want to create such a strong relationship bond that will continue throughout your children's lives that no matter how far they move away from you there will always remain a very strong connection.

Your motto would be, "**to your own self be true.**" Part of your modus operandi as a parent is to find potential in your kids. Your idea is to be the best you can be in every aspect of your life, especially in the parenting role; you encourage your kids to find out what their best is, and then go after it.

As a **nurturer** your preference is to always be there for your kids. One mom told us that she wants their home to be "kid central" for the neighbourhood kids and she is happy to nurture all of her kids' friends as well. She encourages her children to invite friends over for sleepovers, movie days on school holidays, and anything else she can think of to keep them close.

If you take on the Authentic Blue parenting role you not only want to share your **emotions** with your kids, but you expect them to share their feelings too. You tend to be a very "hands-on" parent who wants to touch, hug and demonstrate signs of affection at all times. One mom told us that she thought there was something wrong with her eight-year-old daughter who no longer hugged her every time she left the house!

Mary McGuiness refers to Authentic Blues as "**Catalysts**," and we agree. Parents with the Authentic Blue parenting style, with their focus on the future, naturally motivate their children to find something they love to do, and, hopefully make it their life's goal to make a living from it. With that in mind these parents will read stories to their tiny tots, listen to their teens' dreams, and encourage their offspring to dream about their future endeavours. Your hope is that your children will grow and mature into the adult they were born to be. And you'll be proud that you acted as the spark that led them to finding their niche!

For those with the Authentic Blue parenting preference discipline is difficult because you want to be a friend, a buddy to your kids. You just want everyone to get along and cannot quite fathom why that is not possible. While you may become exasperated with kids when they fight amongst themselves or talking back to you, you just don't really understand the need for battles anywhere — in your own home, or in the world. One parent described the scene of her teen being very argumentative one day; she simply suggested they sit down. She then asked, "What's wrong? Tell me what is really bothering you so we can figure it out together." Clearly, you choose to be more of a **good listener**, and a counsellor when your offspring misbehave.

In summary, those of you who prefer the Authentic Blues' way of parenting believe your parenting role includes one of creating a bond that may lead you to not let go of your kids easily as they grow into maturity. Your nurturing ways will extend throughout their lives as you continue to counsel them in choosing the path that feels right for them, and to feel happy about who they are and about their choices. As one parent described it, "My relationship with my children is one of being a good friend whose grown kids frequently call to make coffee dates!"

Are You on the Resourceful Orange Parenting Journey?

If this is your parenting preference then you are best represented by the **fox**. When we think of a fox he is quick on his feet and can change his direction in an instant. Like the fox, you are constantly on the alert and adaptable to anything that captures your attention. Yours is a busy lifestyle and your family will have to fit around you. One working, marathon-running mom tells us that her five-year-old wakes up early to be with her mom before work to get some "mommy time" as she calls it.

Your motto would fall in line with a bumper sticker we saw from Ben & Jerry's Ice Cream: **"If it's not fun it's not worth doing!"** Your approach to parenthood is likely to be carefree and fun, providing your children with lots of freedom to do what they want, when they want. One mom says, "Life should be fun and I want my kids to enjoy themselves so I take a laissez-faire attitude most of the time. I don't want to cramp their style!"

Part of the fun in life for those of you with the Resourceful Orange parenting style is taking the kids on **adventurous outings**. You encourage your children to be fearless and try new things even if they are a little scared to do so. That might mean lacing up the skates and trying it on their own, without holding on to your hand, when they are preschoolers. As teens you encourage them to take a risk and try for that part time job for which they don't think they have the exact qualifications.

This parenting type enjoys doing many things at once. If anyone enjoys trying to **multi-task** it is the Resourceful Orange! If you are feeling a little bored with life you will add another thing to your already full "to-do" list and be happier for it. For example, one mom described a typical Saturday of running her one child to a birthday party, the other child to a friend's house (in the opposite direction) on the way to her gym class and fitting in a quick shopping trip on the way back to pick up her kids. *"It's all in a day's fun!"* she said, *"I just pack in as much as I can squeeze into a day!"*

Mary McGuiness refers to the Resourceful Oranges as the **Negotiators**; we like to use the word "**Bargainer**" to describe the Resourceful Orange parenting style. We have observed that parents with this preference may bargain with their children with great panache. You will often use this method to get your children to do something, or you may use it to troubleshoot an issue that is going on in the household. For example, one mom told us that her six-year-old child did not want to take her medicine; in fact she was running away from both parents, when mom quickly bargained, "Wouldn't some pixie dust help make the medicine go down easier?" Apparently her child stopped, took the medicine and smiled as mom sprinkled the "pixie dust." There was no real pixie dust! Mom simply used her hand pretending to throw pixie dust and the child loved the play-acting!

Discipline for those with the Resourceful Orange parenting style often takes the form of clever management. A dad told us that he has been known to ask if his teenager would like to drive the car to work in exchange for running an errand that he doesn't particularly want to do! Usually you don't believe in strict boundaries for fear that they will only serve to instill fear into the child. Stephen Montgomery refers to you as the "liberal" parent who prefers to take the **easygoing** and indulgent approach to parenting most of the time. However, as many parents who choose the Resourceful Orange style have told us, if your kid pushes you too far you will take them to task, particularly for any back-talk.

To summarize, Resourceful Oranges' approach their parenting role as an adventure filled with even more interesting things to do. They like to have fun and are somewhat casual when it comes to home life, with few boundaries and a way of bargaining that usually allows them to troubleshoot a number of possible issues hoping that this will result in happy children. They enjoy more of a friendship parenting style.

Are You on the Inquiring Green Parenting Journey?

If this is your parenting preference then you are represented by the **owl**. When we conjure up the image of an owl we think of it sitting independently, as it observes the world from high atop a tree with a knowing look. Like the "wise" owl you enjoy being independent, and somewhat set apart from the rest of the world, even, to some degree, as a parent.

Your motto is "**Let me think about it**." You encourage your children to ponder things in order to encourage their intellectual potential. You relate best with your kids through an intellectual interaction (a discussion, not an argument). You encourage your children to be as competent as possible in their chosen paths; your style is not to choose their paths for them. You also expect your children to set high intellectual standards for themselves, just as you do for yourself.

The Inquiring Green parenting preference would encourage their children to question everything and to seek answers. This is your own method of learning and improving yourself. You try to answer your kids' questions and will also readily direct your children to reference material so they can eventually find answers for themselves. One Inquiring Green parent was observed imparting information to his child who, in the middle of the conversation, asked for the definition of the word the father had just used. The dad immediately provided his child with an excellent definition and then proceeded with the rest of the information.

Your Inquiring Green parenting preference is usually one of **controlled emotions**. Even to your children you may appear to be somewhat cool, reserved and unemotional from time to time. You also tend to be somewhat limited in giving praise to anyone with ease, including your children. In one of our teacher workshops that included a number of Inquiring Green women, they were quick to tell us that as parents they all feel emotion deeply, but are simply not comfortable displaying it frequently, even as mothers. But they did want us all to understand that their emotional ties to their kids are as strong as any other parenting style.

Mary McGuiness refers to Inquiring Greens as **Inventors**. We like to refer to this parenting style as "**Innovators**." If this is your parenting preference you want your children to be innovative, to develop their particular creativity to the fullest, to create a unique individual that is no cookie cutter version of anyone, including their parent. Stephen Montgomery explains that you are hesitant to interfere with your kids "even if they seem to be floundering a bit."[6] You want them to be innovative in finding their own way and eventually become independent and critical thinkers. You want your children to obtain their own information without external manipulation, although you are always ready to help them reach their goals.

Your discipline method is more of a "lecture." You like to use logic in teaching them the importance of thinking about what they did wrong. You like to handle discipline with "**logical consequences**," says David Keirsey. You would argue that whatever children have are privileges and if they abuse the privilege, they lose it. You prefer not to scold, admonish, yell, or even reason with your kids; instead you remove the privilege for a specific time period. Some Inquiring Green parenting types tell us that they say, "Go to your room" to their misbehaving children, which translated, means that you have momentarily removed your child's privilege of being with the family.

In summary, those of you with the Inquiring Greens' approach to parenting take on the role of the intellectual promoter. You want your offspring to be happy and thrive by thinking for themselves, designing their own individual path in life using their maximum intellectual potential. As one father told us, "teaching my son to question in an objective, rather than subjective, way will help him make logical, informed decisions about what matters in life."

And Your Parenting Style Is....

What primary parenting journey are you currently following?

_____

What do you think your secondary style of parenting is?

_____

For those of you who read this chapter and would tell us that you believe you are on the right track that is wonderful! We applaud you! Hopefully this book will help you to maintain a smooth journey.

Alternatively, do you find that while you recognize your style you still feel like your parenting journey needs some help or that it is working well with one child and not as well with another? We hear this all the time. Parents will say things such as, "I've been trying so hard to do what I believe is right but I'm just not getting through to one of my children!"

So what is not working? And what is working? How can *GPS for Navigating Your Kids Personality* help? Next on our journey we will take a look at the strengths and abilities that are innate in each of the four dimensions. As parents you can help your children explore their positive natures.

Chapter 4

GPS FOR YOUR
CHILDREN'S JOURNEY

Sometimes your parenting style seems to work with some or all
of your kids and sometimes that just isn't the case. In any case
you may not be sure why it works or why it doesn't work and many
parents tell us that honestly they have, for the most part, used the
"trial and error" method. But that can bring a lot of stress — for both
the parent and the child.

To alleviate some of the stress, turn back to **Chapter 2:** *Destination:
Disney.* If you figured out the primary personality dimensions of your
children then you are half way to decreasing much of your stress.
Your next piece of information in this *GPS for Navigating Your Kid's
Personality* is simple but for some, mind boggling. Are you ready
for it? All you have to do now is parent to your kid's personality
dimension.

*"What? You mean I have to adjust my parenting style to
accommodate each of my kids?"* asked one mom.

"Yes, you heard correctly," Kate answered.

Kate had realized this through running communication workshops
based on temperament. To communicate effectively participants first
learned the four styles of communication. Then they learned that
by adjusting their preferred communication style to accommodate

another dimension's communication preference their relationship improved. They started to actually listen to one another.

In her parenting workshops Kate started asking parents, for example, if they changed how they spoke to their kids as teenagers from the way they spoke to them when they were two years old. Of course the answer is yes, so without realizing it, the parents had been accommodating their children to a degree. Now, you simply need to change your parenting style to accommodate your children's personality dimension.

If you think of parenting in terms of going to Walt Disney World® Magic Kingdom® Theme Park, this might help you understand what we are saying. For example, if your child had one day in the Magic Kingdom Theme Park® and really loved *Adventureland*®, would you take your child to *Tomorrowland*® instead, insisting that it was the best Land and that your child would love it? You are likely thinking that would just be silly. You want your child to be happy so you would ensure that child would have more time in Adventureland®.

And so it goes with parenting to the styles of your kids. Just as you understand that one child would prefer to visit Adventureland® that child also has a personality dimension with specific strengths and abilities. You can empower them by encouraging them to use their innate strengths and skills to bring them authentic happiness, as discussed in **Chapter 2**. Kate's yoga teacher one day talked about all of us having to "step into our own shoes," as parents we can help our offspring do just that.

The fact is that while you are on your parenting journey, each of your children is on a "growing up" journey of their own. As their primary caretaker you are in a wonderful position to help them develop their innate **strengths**.

It is fascinating to look back over the centuries to find that a Renaissance physician, from Vienna, Paracelsus,[1] described the four personality types in terms of strengths. He used different names of course, but essentially he stated that the Organized Golds are industrious and guarded, Authentic Blues are inspired and passionate, Resourceful Oranges are impulsive and changeable; while the Inquiring Greens are curious and calm. Here we are five centuries later still agreeing with his synopsis!

Have you ever had someone tell you that you possess a certain ability that you take for granted and don't think a lot about? That is probably because it is your innate talent. Using your knowledge of your child's particular colour preference, you are in the unique position of possibly being the one to introduce them to their inborn **abilities**, and to help them develop these talents over their growing years in a positive way.

Every child has the potential to be **"*the little engine that could;*"** as parents you can help your offspring reach their goals by constantly reminding them of their strong points. In fact, Seligman recommends that parents "reward all displays of any of the strengths ... (and to) go out of your way to allow your child to display (them).[2] This, in turn, will raise their self esteem and prepare them to face their world with confidence, with assurance, and a belief that they can succeed.

Let's see how you can help your children develop their innate strengths and abilities positively, while raising their self esteem so they can become *"the little engine that could"* and so experience authentic happiness[3].

GPS for Organized Golds

Organized Golds' Strengths

On the May 24 long weekend, so the story goes, a couple discovered that their plumbing issues stemmed from the roots of the old tree at the side of their house. What a mess when that tree came down! The parents and some of their friends started to drag the limbs off the grass to a pile for pick-up later. Their eight-year-old child watched the adults for a few minutes and then began to help clear the branches off very methodically, always choosing manageable branches to carry. Their child continued to work alongside the adults until the job was done.

This story encapsulates many of the strengths of Organized Golds, which actually start at a much younger age than even eight years. Let's see how...

These children are **willing to help**. They see a need and often provide assistance, like this child who began methodically working alongside the parents, without being asked to do so. They see it as a way of belonging to their family and contributing in a positive manner. It is a way for them to relate to their families, to their extended families, and later to their communities. The Organized Gold children also enjoy family reunions of any sort and will help to make them happen.

Organized Golds **get things done** and usually in an efficient manner. They like to take on projects that have a beginning, middle, and an end. This young Organized Gold could see all the branches that needed to be moved and set about to get it done. The child picked up the ones that were not too heavy and continued to do so until all of the branches were out of the way.

Meeting deadlines within a specific time frame is a strength that Organized Golds possess. In this case the family wanted the tree branches at the curb that day, ready for garbage pick-up. Then they would order take-out. To meet that deadline the little Organized Gold continued to work at clearing the branches in time for dinner! In this case it was doable in a reasonable period of time; in some cases parents may need to monitor their Organized Gold children and encourage them to take a few breaks.

Organized Golds usually **create order** as they work. In this scenario the child looked at the sizes of the branches and only moved the ones small enough to carry. In addition, this Organized Gold did not try to carry a lot of branches at one time nor increase the workload by taking only tiny twigs. The child also placed the branches in piles, according to their size.

Within this story you can see that there was **careful thinking before the actual doing**. Organized Golds will assess the situation to see what needs to be done before beginning the task. If they are not sure about doing it they may ask you HOW. In this scenario the Organized Gold child first observed the adults moving the tree branches and then began to help.

Organized Golds **care about the details**. They learn best when shown a new skill in a step-by-step order. Once they have these details then they know what they are expected to do and are usually happy to go about doing it. These personality types enjoy making lists and checking off each item once they have completed it. In this scenario, the child placed the small twigs in one pile and the bigger ones in another pile.

Organized Golds have a **clear sense of right and wrong**. This child, for example, clearly had an idea of how many branches it was possible to carry at a time and set about getting it done. It was also clear to this Organized Gold that it was the right thing to do — to help the adults with this big project. Remember that these are the kids who like rules and want to follow them. They believe there is a right way of doing things and want to plan how to do it correctly.

Organized Golds' Talents

The adjective used to describe each of the colour groups reflects the overall skill of that group. In the case of Organized Golds their overall talent is one of planning and organizing. Something your kids may enjoy doing and would be very good at is planning and organizing parties and events for the family. Let's see how planning a simple event showcases a Gold child's abilities.

If you ask an Organized Gold child (or teen) to help plan an ordinary Friday night family night with their extended family members (i.e., siblings, cousins) they may propose food that would be appreciated, specific games to play and maybe even prizes for the winners! Planning is fun for Organized Golds.

Organized Golds are naturally skilled at **taking care of the details**. To help plan this Friday night event, they would very likely create a list of activities for the party. They may decide to offer a variety of beverages when their cousins arrive, then play a game before serving dinner. Afterwards it might be a movie, followed by dessert, and then maybe awarding prizes to the winners.

Their innate ability to **collect and sort information** comes in handy at this point. They can collect ideas for the drinks, the game, the dinner, the movie, the dessert and the prizes. Once they have lists of collections, they will be able to sort through the long list to create the exact list of foods, drinks, etc., that they will offer.

They tend to be very good at **paying attention**. That being the case, they likely have a good idea of the foods, games, and movies the family members enjoy. They would be collecting and sorting the information based on their knowledge of likes and dislikes within the group to ensure that everyone enjoys the party.

Many Organized Golds are talented at **bookkeeping and accounting**. In the case of the party you might want to provide them with a budget if that is age appropriate. That way they will know, for example, whether they should consider buying a cake or making one at home.

If Organized Golds are not old enough to understand bookkeeping the good news is that children with this personality preference are good at **following directions**. If you told them that we need to be careful with the spending they would listen to your direction and choose to bake the cake rather than buy one from the bakery, for example.

The day of the party Organized Golds may surprise you by how well they can **manage** the event. If they know what the plan is for the party they will want to at least help manage it! If the plan is to have drinks then a game, they will probably make sure that everyone has had a drink before they start playing games.

The Little Engine That Could:
Raising Organized Golds' Self Esteem

Organized Golds' self esteem rises when they feel that they are **dependable**. They take on the responsibility of routine jobs around the house, such as emptying the garbage, setting the table, raking, shoveling, etc. An interesting note here is that Seligman maintains that parents "design the chores around the kids' differing strengths"[4] and that "having chores as a child is one of the only early predictors of positive mental health later in life!"[5] Make sure the chores are age-appropriate. These are the children who like routine maintenance. When they are finished the task make sure you recognize what a great job they have done. One parent told us that their Organized Gold child is happy when they simply say something like *"thanks for feeding the cat without getting any of her food on the floor!"*

Organized Golds often grow up to serve their community (e.g., teachers, police, or public servants).[6] This colour feels good about themselves when they can **serve others**, whether they are preschoolers or teenagers. So let them help plan family holidays, parties, do household tasks, or help with younger siblings. One new mom told us that her Organized Gold toddler loved helping mommy by running to get a diaper for her baby sister, and it sure helped mommy out! That same toddler grew up to be the teenager who drove the younger sibling to the doctor's office during the day so the working parents didn't have to take time off work to do it.

Organized Golds stand up taller when they receive **visible recognition** of work well done. That may translate into a job chart at home, especially for the younger children. For every job they do they receive a sticker or a star on the chart. They can then show this chart off with pride since their service to the family is being visibly recognized. As they get older this may translate into earning the right to use the family car on the weekend.

Organized Golds like to have things in **order**. Part of being organized is having your life in order for this personality dimension. You will see this from a very young child who wants an orderly play area, so if you provide bins for their various toys, and show them how to use them, they will put their toys away. As they grow older they want order in their schedule of events so they know what they are doing each day of the week, after school and on the weekend. You can help them feel in control of their lives by planning the week's schedule with them and sticking to it. This becomes very important to the teen who will have homework, extra-curricular activities and possibly part time jobs to juggle.

In summary, we can see why the Viennese doctor from the 1500s called this personality type "industrious." Organized Golds are very hard workers, but they can get so caught up in the work that even as children they may forget to play or take breaks! As you know from **Chapter 3**, we often use the beaver as a symbol for this dimension. With a little help from you your Organized Gold child can become dependable adults who help maintain order in our society!

GPS for Authentic Blues

Authentic Blues' Strengths

At the age of 12 a Pakistani boy named Iqbal Masik, a slave in a carpet factory, was murdered. At the age of 12 a Canadian boy

*named Craig Kielburger responded by forming an organization
called "Free the Children," an international network of children with
the one mission: eradicate world-wide child slave labour. Craig, his
family, and his school chums, raised funds by holding garage sales,
car washes, bake sales, etc. I remember watching this teen on TV
as he travelled to South Asia at 14 to find enslaved children. Not
everyone agreed with him but he continued with his mission. As
an adult he and his brother, Marc, both dedicated activists, have
built this organization into one that has initiated world-wide projects,
opening over 100 schools and rehab centres for exploited children.
They also founded "Leaders Today," an organization to teach
leadership skills and to empower children worldwide[7].*

Although we have only had the pleasure of meeting his brother
Marc, Craig Kielburger's story captures the essential strengths of the
Authentic Blues. Let's see how...

Authentic Blues **show their true concerns**, even at a very young
age. In the case of Kielburger, he began raising money for kids his
own age who could not speak out for themselves. He didn't stop at
making it a class project in his eighth grade, which is how he started,
but continued to show concern by travelling to Asia, using funds
he had helped raise. He was certainly a child with a cause who
demonstrated the power of one!

Their **commitment to helping people** may be displayed in smaller
ways than Craig Kielburger's by the majority of Authentic Blues.
It may be simply by continuing to be a good pal, or a support to
someone who needs a friend when their families are experiencing a
rough time. Many parents tell us that their Authentic Blue children
like to help friends with homework, or help their parents in various
ways, such as looking after younger siblings.

Authentic Blues exercise **creative thinking**. Craig Kielburger
created a not-for-profit organization in order to fund his mission at
a very young age. We have heard of other young friends who have
helped raise funds for cancer by cutting their own hair and selling it.

There was another young Authentic Blue-type heroine on the news who, with a little duct tape and a lot of creativity began making and selling wallets to raise funds for friends who suffer from a rare syndrome.

The Authentic Blues' natural strength of **sharing thoughts** with others is clearly illustrated in the life of Kielburger. Like many other children in this dimension, as a youngster, he was very able to articulate his concern, and his solutions to his family, and to his entire class. We often think of this colour in terms of emotions, which is true, but they also have the strength to think through their emotions and communicate their thoughts quite eloquently. Many motivational speakers share this personality dimension with Kielburger, who himself is an inspirational, thoughtful speaker.

You may find your Authentic Blue children **work well with others**. It is no surprise that, given their penchant for good relationships and harmonious environments, they would strive to work in such a way with others that they would help create cooperation. We can only imagine that twelve-year-old Kielburger managed to do so as he raised funding, and continues to do so today as an adult!

These children are often about **helping others grow**. Tom Maddron tells us that they "root for the underdog."[8] In this example, Kielburger could easily have moved on after his initial project with his school mates at the age of 12. Instead he continues to raise funds and awareness for children world-wide. No doubt his Leaders Today organization helps many children grow and feel empowered.

Authentic Blues enjoy **building harmony** at home, at school, in the community, and later, at work. Twelve-year-old Kielburger demonstrated the strength in the Authentic Blue dimension when he stated his belief that no child anywhere in the world should be a slave. Then, as now, he wanted to build harmony around the world, one dollar at a time. Authentic Blues not only desire, but will often stand up for, a harmonious world, even if they do not ever get the kind of recognition that Craig Kielburger has received.

Authentic Blues' Talents

As you can see we describe this dimension as "authentic," meaning genuine and sincere. We often say that in their case "what you see is what you get," with no hidden agendas. This group wants be the best that they can be through helping and nurturing others. Let's see how an Authentic Blue child uses natural abilities.

One parent tells the story of their eleven-year old Authentic Blue whose sibling feared walking on bridges over water. While visiting Boston, family members wanted to walk over the bridge from one side of the city to the other side. The Authentic Blue put an arm around the sibling and said, "C'mon I'll help you get across. We can do this together." The Authentic Blue then proceeded to walk on the outer side shielding the sibling's view of the water. The two walked arm-in-arm safely over the bridge without a whimper on the part of the younger child.

Authentic Blues naturally **mediate conflicts**. In this case, the Authentic Blue recognized that the other family members could easily have been agitated and say something unkind to the child who did not want to walk across the bridge. The immediate reaction of this sincere Authentic Blue child was to jump in before any true conflict occurred and solve the problem.

You can see that **encouraging others** is part of their innate ability too. The simple act of putting an arm around the frightened sibling served to encourage that child to lean on the other one. It was the one sibling saying to the other that together they would and could make it across to the other side of the bridge.

This is a good illustration of the Authentic Blue ability to **motivate** people to do something they don't necessarily want to do themselves. With the simple word, "c'mon" the Authentic Blue is able to stimulate the other to take one step forward on the bridge, and many steps later, find themselves on the other side of the bridge.

Many Authentic Blues grow up to become therapists, guidance counsellors, motivational speakers, psychologists, primary school teachers, etc. because they are good at **listening and communicating**. A simple example like this vignette demonstrates that an eleven-year-old listened to their sibling's fears and acted upon them by communicating to that sibling that getting to the other side was doable.

Their innate **mentoring and training** skills help Authentic Blues counsel others throughout their lives, even as children. By helping their sibling get across to the other side, this Authentic Blue demonstrated how to conquer a somewhat fearful situation through positive action. Hopefully when faced with another anxious situation the Authentic Blue has both mentored and trained this younger sibling to realize the possibility of conquering future fears.

Authentic Blues strive to **maintain harmony** at home, at school, in the playground, and later in the workforce. In this little vignette the Authentic Blue recognized potential conflict and nipped it in the bud by taking the sibling under their wing right away and maintained the cohesiveness of the family outing.

The Little Engine That Could:
Raising Authentic Blues' Self Esteem

Not all Authentic Blue children receive formal recognition of any kind for their acts of kindness. But all Authentic Blue children do receive a boost in confidence when their parents provide them with **personal recognition for their accomplishments**. One parent whose child is not a straight-A student does something special with her offspring if her child's report card reflects working up to her potential. The activities have varied according to the age of the child, but it is made clear that this is to recognize the personal accomplishment in that semester.

Authentic Blues thrive in a **harmonious environment** with congenial relationships at home, at school, and later at work. Tom Maddron[9] goes as far as to say that they would choose harmony over success. One parent disclosed that her child will draw beautiful pictures when their household is filled with "good vibes," but will often "draw a blank" when there is any disharmony, even if it is just siblings disagreeing in another room.

Authentic Blues grow in confidence when given **opportunity to communicate with, to support, and to encourage others**. For example, an Authentic Blue adult tells us that as a child who won a speech contest in the classroom and then in the school, and then in the city, it gave them great confidence to speak in public. The adult is now a speaker, a workshop leader and a coach who is communicating with, supporting and encouraging others.

Something that boosts the confidence of Authentic Blues is pleasing others. From a very young age they like to be given the **opportunity to please**. One parent tells us that their Authentic Blue loved giving them gifts even as a very young child — with money earned by the child, often through extra chores around the home.

As Dr. Paracelsus from Vienna indicated, these children are inspired and passionate. Whether it is a 12-year-old who uses his "power of one" or the little Authentic Blue in your household, with your help they may just change the world and make it a more peaceful place in which to live!

GPS for Resourceful Oranges

Resourceful Oranges' Strengths

One couple tells the story of their Resourceful Orange teenager who had grown up in a church where annually a group of teens would travel to a third-world country to help out. By the time their *teen was old enough the church had stopped this practice. So the Resourceful Orange researched and found an American group that was travelling to a French-speaking country in Africa to build a school in a remote village. The first major hurdle the teen encountered was convincing the parents that a stint with strangers in a strange country for six weeks was a good idea. The second hurdle was raising $4000 for the trip, which was accomplished just in time; the teen babysat, ran errands, held several garage sales, etc. It turned out that this teen was only one of two teens able to speak French with the Africans, thus taking on the role of translator. This Resourceful Orange enjoyed chatting to the African people in their language about their lives.*

This story encapsulates many of the strengths of Resourceful Oranges. Let's see how...

Resourceful Oranges **see opportunities** where others might miss them. In this case, the teen watched the teenagers before her and saw a great opportunity to be free from parents and routines of home (for a short period) while at the same time doing something for others and being applauded for doing good works!

They tend to be very good **problem solvers**, hence the adjective in front of their colour is "resourceful." Many teens would have given up the notion of going to a third world country when their church discontinued the program. But not this one, who researched and contacted a number of similar groups to find the right fit, one that included a French component, allowing the teen to practice a second language all summer.

You will often notice that Resourceful Oranges are **flexible and relaxed**. In fact they enjoy change so much that it usually doesn't matter to them if something doesn't work out as planned. More often than not they just don't care that there is a change, and remain relaxed when a challenging situation comes up. In this case it worked to the teen's advantage to be only one of two French-speaking students since they became the translators for the group; a role this teen thoroughly enjoyed!

These kids are up for a challenge and will work **long and hard** to achieve something they set their minds to do. They may want to become very good at playing a sport, or playing an instrument, or writing a story. In this case it was about getting on a plane to fly half way around the world to experience a whole new world. It meant many hours spent accruing the funds but it paid off when the teen had enough cash to travel.

In fact, Resourceful Oranges **work well under pressure**. These are the kids who usually leave projects and studying until the last minute. But once they make up their mind to get to work they will get it done! This teen worked right up to the last minute to accumulate the $4000 required. The parents did divulge that they had been willing to "kick in" a shortfall if required, but they knew their child well enough that they were sure the money would be earned. They were right. At the eleventh hour the teen had the required funding!

Resourceful Oranges are generally up for a challenge and can usually **think quickly**. That is one reason they do well in team sports and in public speaking where they have to "think on their feet." This teen's parents threw up many roadblocks initially to test their child's true desire to actually secure the funding and use their whole summer vacation to build a school in Africa. But their child capably provided both quick and relevant answers to their many questions.

Finally, one of the strengths that many Resourceful Oranges exhibit is to be both **fun and entertaining**. Kate always says that she thinks "fun" is their middle name because they seem to see the fun in so many things and they have a knack for making even the mundane seem enjoyable and entertaining. This teen travelled to a remote village and yet came home with the most entertaining stories of sitting under the large trees and having tea with the elder African villagers while teammates built the school under the hot sun. This teen found the fun in the villagers' stories and spent many hours later relaying some of them. If asked about Africa this child's response is apparently a broad grin, exclaiming, "Oh it was so much fun!"

Resourceful Oranges' Talents

The adjective used to describe the Orange personality is resourceful, which according to the dictionary is having the ability to find quick and clever ways to overcome difficulties. Let's see how one Resourceful Orange quickly figured out how to get out of an immensely disliked chore.

In recalling her Resourceful Orange child, this mother remembers that her child enjoyed creativity in the kitchen and was very good at cooking. So when it came time to clean and paint this young teen's room the Resourceful Orange who did not like sorting, cleaning or painting suggested a deal: the parents and siblings do the work in the bedroom in exchange for three scrumptious meals prepared by this budding chef. At the end of the day the other family members raved about the delicious and creative meals, and the Resourceful Orange had a cleaned, organized, newly-painted room. Everyone was happy — especially the teen!

Resourceful Oranges are very talented at "**making deals.**" This one negotiated a newly cleaned-up and freshly-painted bedroom in exchange for cooking three meals. Some Resourceful Oranges grow up to be negotiators, sales people, stockbrokers or entrepreneurs, all of whom "make deals." Often their rooms can get quite disorganized over time and Resourceful Oranges tell us they generally like it if someone helps by sorting out the "junk" and cleaning. This Resourceful Orange realized that sorting, cleaning and painting the bedroom would involve unenjoyable work, but creating the meals would be much more fun.

Convincing other people is a natural talent that you will see in Resourceful Oranges. It may start at a very young age when you find yourself agreeing to let the Resourceful Orange stay up later than you had planned, or have more time to play, or later, extend their curfew. In this little vignette, the teen convinced the family that they needed someone to cook so they could continue to sort, clean, and paint uninterrupted. All they had to do was sit down to a wonderful meal!

Driving something to action is a skill that comes naturally to the Resourceful Orange so at an early age they will often take charge to get it done and get on to the next thing. Apparently this Resourceful Orange enjoyed taking charge of the kitchen and enjoyed the opportunity of cooking all three meals that day without supervision from parents, who were busy in another room in the house. For those of you who may be worried, this teen had grown up cooking with both parents so it was not dangerous. Needless to say, had this teen chosen to help clean and paint the bedroom her parents would have been in charge!

Creating and designing things allow Resourceful Oranges to utilize their physical skills. In this vignette the teen was given "carte blanche" to cook three "scrumptious" meals for the day; the teen enjoyed total freedom to create and design three different meals using herbs and spices and ingenuity to provide the family with a wonderful culinary experience.

Part of the resourcefulness of this group includes **"getting things done."** In this example, the teen figured out a way to get the bedroom sorted, cleaned and painted without ever having to go into the room. This teen wanted nothing to do with that kind of work but was delighted to exchange it for creating meals and being chef for the day — something that was most appealing apparently!

Performing comes easily to the Resourceful Orange dimension. They often demonstrate what they can do at a very young age. This is the child who may pick up a trumpet and be able to play a note right away, or the child who scores in hockey or in soccer at a young age, or the teen who shows wonderful photography skills and wins a school contest. In our scenario the Resourceful Orange wanted to demonstrate excellent cooking skills and so happily suggested becoming chef for the day for the family, perhaps a prelude to a career as a professional chef some day!

The Little Engine That Could:
Raising Resourceful Oranges' Self Esteem

Resourceful Oranges want the **freedom to express themselves** in their own way. As a parent you need to decide to what extent you might allow that freedom of expression, yet it can be a way to rebuild their self confidence. One mom tells us that her youngster watched her get ready for work by applying makeup; the child wanted to model her mom. They bought her a make-up kit, which she loves to use at home, with the caveat that she not put make-up on before school. She and her girlfriends often play "mommy getting ready for work" together.

These children **love an audience**, even it if is an audience of one — you! Taking a few minutes to play ball with them, to hear them play their latest piece of music, or to ask them about a picture they have drawn goes a long way to raising their self esteem. The child in the last example had her mom tape, and post, a video of her describing the art of giving a manicure. She loved showing off her abilities. Naturally the video was sent to extended family members and close friends who then "oohed and aahed" as well.

Spontaneity is very important to Resourceful Oranges. Allowing them to act on impulse, in the moment, allows them to feel confident about this trait. For parents who want to plan and manage schedules, you may have to be like the willow tree and bend a little. Or, as one parent divulged, build spontaneity into the schedule so their Resourceful Orange never guessed that it wasn't a spur of the moment decision to go to the mall or go visit friends or have ice cream cake for dessert!

Letting the Resourceful Oranges **take risks** helps build their self-esteem. As babies, Resourceful Oranges will often try climbing the stairs long before their siblings do; let them, but just follow behind to catch them. These energetic kids might want to enter a race before you think they are ready for it; let them. Just remember not to judge them if they don't quite succeed at something because they will simply move on to the next adventure and keep on trying until they do succeed!

The good doctor from Vienna clearly indicated that this personality dimension can be impulsive and changeable. As parents of Resourceful Oranges you will likely find it challenging and hopefully a lot of fun — never quite knowing what is next, but always trying to support the adventurous spirit!

GPS for Inquiring Greens

Inquiring Greens' Strengths

From the time he was not much more than a toddler our child showed a fascination with tools and how they work, using them to both take things apart and put them back together. At the age of four or five our child was helping me renovate — not just fetching tools and watching me work, but actually doing things. By age eight our child was fixing mountain bikes, learning how they worked by first stripping them down and then rebuilding them. But it was at the age of six when our child was first introduced to computers that, looking back, we realized that this was to become a lifelong passion. Although this child picked it all up fast, his real joy was the hardware side and what made them work. At the age of nine he was given a computer and from then on made all the computer upgrades with no help from us or from experts. In high school this same child worked for a fellow that sold computer systems and, you guessed it, it was this teenager who built them by the dozen every week as a part-time job!

This story took place in the early 1990s when computers were not in every household and not many children had any kind of device yet; the story encapsulates many of the strengths of the Inquiring Greens, starting at a very young age. Let's see how...

Figuring out "how" and "why" something works seems to be part of Inquiring Greens' DNA! They will ask questions incessantly because they are preoccupied with how and why things work. In this case the child had a propensity for tools at a very young age. But the child didn't just want to play with or hold them as many kids at this age would have been happy to do. Instead, this little Inquiring Green wanted to explore how the tools were made and why they worked in specific ways; the one way to discover that is to take the tools apart and put them back together. In this case the youngster was actually successful in putting them together exactly the way they were made!

Learning fascinates Inquiring Greens as long as they can choose the project, set their goals, and work with little supervision. When something interests them they want to learn more and more about the subject. In our vignette, the child learned by examining, taking apart and putting together the tools, the bikes and the computers. We should probably add a caveat here. Inquiring Greens generally prefer to learn about what interests them, which may not include every subject at school. Indeed we have had more than one Inquiring Green tell us that it seems like a waste of time learning about something that you may never need to access in your future!

In our vignette, the Inquiring Green **works hard on the projects**. In this case it is a fascination with tools, specifically computers, that ends up becoming a part-time job. When asked if his child was a student who achieved high marks, the answer was "no," this child preferred working diligently on chosen projects, which were not always school related.

Thinking is important to the Inquiring Greens and **clear thinking** is something they admire and work towards. They are logical and objective kids who, while they tend not to express emotions very often, use most of their time to think things through clearly. T his child clearly thought through how to take apart and put together computers.

Inquiring Greens will work hard in order to **understand the meaning** of things. They think logically and want things to make sense. From a young age the child in our story had a passion for tools that superseded anything else in life. The youngster worked to understand them so well that it led to the job of building them!

Inquiring Greens naturally **think about ideas**. They ask the question, "What if ...?" and then begin to answer their own questions and are delighted if you join in, almost turning it into a game! They like new ideas. They think about concepts, systems, technology in new ways that allow them to formulate new ideas to think about, to explore, to imagine. If you remember, one of our Inquiring Green groups, for example, came up with the idea of travelling to Mars as a holiday, before it was ever a reality. The child in our story grew up to create innovative computer hardware systems.

Using exactly the right word is something the Inquiring Greens insist upon. While this was not illustrated in the example above, upon further questioning, the father adamantly agreed that his child would stop to correct anyone if they thought there was a better, or a right word, to use. He added that his child, now an adult, continues to introduce him to new concepts and insists on dad using the correct terminology in their discussions.

We think you will agree with our good Viennese doctor in the 1500s who described this personality type as "curious." They never stop asking questions and learning about things. Sometimes they find it difficult to stop thinking long enough to sleep!

Inquiring Greens' Talents

The adjective used to describe each of the personality dimensions reflects the overall talents of this group. In the case of the

Inquiring Greens their overall gift is one of inquiring and analyzing. Something they love to do and tend to be very good at is technology. Here is a story of another Inquiring Green child during the early 1990s whose abilities are quite recognizable:

My child's interest simmered for a couple of years and then in Grade 7 this one just dived into computer programming, spending hard-earned savings to buy a good used computer, learning to type 80 words per minute in about a week and never looked back. My teen was doing website creation for a small company in Grade 9, being self-taught in animation, etc. This kid worked for a big computer outfit as part of a co-op portion in Grade 12 and was subsequently hired by them as an animator/programmer at the end of that year, earning a very good salary.

Inquiring Greens have an innate desire and ability to **analyze** and then **solve problems**. The very young kids want busy boards, Lego, puzzles, construction sets, and a little later chemistry sets, microscopes and electronics. This child of the 1990s found a life-long passion in grade seven: computer software and programming. Other careers he may have chosen in the tech field might include astronomer, astrophysicist, chemist or pilot. They are good at discovering the root of a problem because they tend to be "free thinkers;" they want to think without restriction of time or space or methodology.

You can tell that the Inquiring Greens tend to make plans from this little vignette. Here the child plans to buy a computer with money earned; the youngster plans to be able to use the keyboard by learning to type at a fast speed, and then plans a future in software by learning animation without a teacher!

Inquiring Greens need to **create a mental picture** in order to build a Lego figure, or new software, or formulate a scientific theorem. That is why they are good at strategic mental games like chess or Mastermind where they have a mental picture of future moves. This could lead to careers in many areas, including architecture, as

a composer or writer. They often "see" your move ahead of you!
Our example depicts a child who created mental pictures, such as
animation, and later, a job in a related field.

The Inquiring Greens' calm nature helps them in their natural
inclination to **observe**. In our example the Inquiring Green was
able to observe how animation worked and then learned to do it
independently, without a teacher or a coach. They generally prefer
to observe the problem at hand and work it out on their own, rather
than ask for instructions or directions, although they are often happy
to learn from others with expertise in the area through research or
conversation.

As an extension of their problem solving abilities, Inquiring Greens
enjoy **researching and developing**. The child in our sample
researched animation extensively on-line. Inquiring Greens enjoy
researching information on topics they find interesting and then
developing their own "take" on the topic of interest. When they
give you an opinion it is usually the result of having researched the
subject and developed their own ideas. It is for this reason that they
enjoy debating ideas with you.

The more difficult the idea, the more fascinating it is for Inquiring
Greens. They will work hard at **understanding difficult ideas**.
The concept of computer programming may be hard to master for
some of us, but for this child in the early 1990s it was a challenge to
understand a difficult concept such as animation and then use that
knowledge to develop new software; clearly this Inquiring Green met
the challenge!

**The Little Engine That Could:
Raising Inquiring Greens' Self Esteem**

Inquiring Greens are born to be **curious**! Help them in their quest
to learn, to figure out how and why things work. We know it isn't
always easy but be patient and answer their constant questions. As

they grow older you can direct them to resources to find answers to their questions for themselves!

Help them feel competent, feel intelligent, **feel "smart."** Remember, they seek knowledge and want to appear knowledgeable. So while you may challenge them with a difficult puzzle, for example, don't make it so hard that they cannot figure it out. David Keirsey[10] reminds us that these are the children most vulnerable to self-doubt and believing they are not smart enough. These are the kids that want you to recognize them for their good ideas, their intelligence.

Allow them space and time to be **autonomous**, to be independent from you, at least to some degree. They will insist upon their independence from a very young age. For example, young Inquiring Greens may want to dress themselves or put on their own boots — even if it takes them a long time to do so. They want to figure out school problems by themselves; they may want to work on High School projects without your input. It may be difficult, but we often suggest that you step away and let your Inquiring Green ask you for help when they want it, that way they don't feel manipulated or managed. These are the kids who declare their independence long before many parents are ready to give it!

Along with the desire to be independent is the need to be an **individual**. It is not in their nature to conform to the norms of society, or to particularly be concerned about the family traditions and routines. They want to think things through for themselves and come to their own individual conclusions. They will often question the authority of their parent, their teacher, and, later on, their boss; holding them all to a very high standard. Allow them to think for themselves, to develop into the individual Inquiring Green who may or may not choose to join in the communal routines and customs.

One way to help the Inquiring Greens develop their individuality is to introduce them to **stories of heroes and heroines** through movies, videos, and books. These are the kids whose goals are to achieve high intellectual standards for themselves. They are thrilled with stories of the exploits of heroic figures. Stephen Montgomery[11] suggests that their interests may include science fiction, fantasy, tales of magic and sorcery, and mysteries. In our family, for example, most of the Inquiring Greens enjoy movies such as *Star Wars™, Harry Potter,* and the *SuperHeroes.*

In the words of our Renaissance Viennese doctor, the Inquiring Green dimension is curious and calm. If you can be patient while answering their many questions and appreciate their quiet, individualistic spirit you may very well raise a deep thinker who will contribute something new and innovative to society.

Now that we have taken a look at the strengths, the abilities and the self esteem of each colour dimension, what about the stresses? What are the "bumps in the road" along the journey for each of the four personality dimensions? Let's have a look in the next chapter.

Chapter 5

GPS FOR "BUMPS" ALONG THE WAY

You are half way through your parenting journey with us and we hope you have picked up some *"Great Parenting Skills"* for all four personality dimensions, but alas, the reality is that we live in a less-than-perfect world. So your offspring will experience stressors, which may be in the form of external events, or from their own innate personality dimension stressors. What happens if rather than feeling good and having a successful day, the opposite happens? In two words: Stress Attack! Or, as we like to call it, *bumps along the way*.

And really, can anyone say that there are no *bumps along the way* in every journey? They might be such small bumps that they barely jiggle you. Or they might be potholes that make your stomach do cartwheels when you pass through them. Either way, *bumps along the way* in the context of this book are very specific to each dimension pattern.

What? Did we say that each of the four natures experiences its own type of "bump" - er - stress?

Yes! In fact, we agree with Mary McGuiness, the author of *You've Got Personality*, who says that "personality differences have a major impact on the way we experience stress and on how we respond to it."[1]

So, in addition to the stress that our children experience in our fast-paced society they also experience stress specific to their natures?

Yes! And to add to your distress as parents, according to Linda Berens, stress "is worse when it is unconscious!"[2] So hidden tension, based on innate nature, may be affecting your children's behaviour and emotions, and they don't know it.

That's the bad news.

Ready for the good news? We have three sections for each colour, or personality dimension group to help you understand the *bumps along the way*.

First, how do you know whether your children are dealing with unconscious stressors that are part of their innate nature? In our neck of the woods new road signs appeared over the winter that read, "Operators raise your plow here" for the snowplow drivers since the snow covers the installed speed bumps that serve to slow drivers down. With snow-covered roads, the plow operators would not know there were hidden bumps without the sign indicating their existence. We like to think of these covered speed bumps as a metaphor for the unconscious stressors, and the warning sign as a metaphor for what we are going to call your *radar detection* section of that unconscious dimension stress.

Secondly, having knowledge of what we refer to as the *bumps encountered* section for each dimension can help you "manage and even prevent such stress."[3] Knowing these common stressors reminds us of caution signs posted on the street warning of a bump ahead, preparing us for the jolt before we see the bump. This section prepares you for the possible "jolts," namely personality dimension stressors, to look for in each of the four colours.

Finally, now that you know the signs to look for and the actual stressors of each dimension, you might be asking, "What can I do to help alleviate the stress?" Don't worry! We provide you with the antidotes in the *smoothing out* section for each group.

So let's carry on with your parenting journey. First have your radar detection ready to observe your kids' stress signs along the journey. Then be ready to see what bumps each dimension might encounter. Finally let's explore some antidotes for those stressors in smoothing the bumps.[4]

GPS for BUMPS in the Organized Golds' Journey

Radar Detection for Organized Golds' Stress

How do you detect the presence of stress in Organized Gold children? What does distress look like for them? Being both dependable and reliable, the Organized Golds will generally focus on completing their tasks with a serious attitude, following the rules and respecting both you and their teachers. However, on a less-than-perfect day you may detect the opposite in your Organized Golds!

They may be **complaining and irritable** far more than usual or perhaps feeling sorry for themselves. For example, they may have a great relationship with their siblings and suddenly be complaining about every little thing they are doing. Or, they may be telling you that they don't think they are very good and shouldn't be on a team anymore, even though they have always enjoyed being on it.

These normally responsible children may act irresponsibly, **refusing to cooperate**. If they have specific tasks to do around the house they won't do them, or they start "fooling around" instead of getting down to work. If asked about it they may answer flippantly "I'll do it later," or just shrug their shoulders.

When Organized Golds exhibit **more anxiety and worry than usual** you know they are stressed. Maybe in the past they have expressed concern over getting good marks in exams or on a term test, but now they are displaying far more anxiety over a small quiz. Perhaps they have always set the table and now express anxiety about having too many chores and not enough time to finish everything.

They may exhibit a very **authoritarian**, overly **judgemental attitude**. They may say something like, "I don't think the coach makes those other kids practice enough and has no idea what he is doing. I told him that we need to practice at least two hours every time but I know he doesn't want to bother figuring out good moves, and he won't listen to my ideas which are much better!"

This dimension usually has the most common sense of all the groups. When your kid seems to **lose their common sense** then you know they are stressed. Perhaps your teenager wants to add another commitment to an already busy schedule. When you suggest that doing two things at once is not possible, the teen keeps telling you that both ball practice and band are important and a "must do" on the to-do list, even though they are both scheduled at the same time.

This group generally likes to take control of their lives. When they start to take on a **"herd mentality"** and blindly follow a leader then clearly something is bothering them. For example, a child may say something like, "I want those shoes because Joey and everyone else is wearing them" or a teen, who normally doesn't like swimming very much, may say, "Leslie, and all of my friends are on the swim team so I'm joining too, no matter what you say!"

Finally, you might notice physical symptoms that set off your radar, such as **fatigue** or even getting sick more often. For example, they don't want to get out of bed in the morning, when usually they are the first ones up. Or they drag themselves out of bed and want nothing to eat, saying they are too tired to bother, or even sick.

"Bumps" Encountered in the Organized Golds' Journey

Here's a little reminder: Organized Golds' core needs include feeling like they belong to the family, which they display through taking on duties and responsibilities. Some of their values include security, traditions, rules, details, plans, and finishing what they start.

If you turn the good things upside down and have a look at what happens when their day doesn't go well, you'll soon recognize the stressors in your children's lives, at least from the point of view of their natures.

If you think about the word ORGANIZED as the descriptor for the Golds then anything that is "DIS-organized" acts as a stressor. Let's see what we mean...

Organized Golds may take on a lot of responsibility and manage it well. However, they can and do take on more commitments that they can humanly handle sometimes. It is called **over-commitment.** When Kate says this in a seminar invariably the Organized Gold parents will nod their heads in agreement. Some verbally acknowledge that this is the case, saying something like, "I just don't know what to do." These are adults. Imagine the stress going on in your youngsters. They try to do 100% in schoolwork, at home, and in extracurricular activities. Two high school administrators confirmed in a workshop that often it is the Organized Golds who take on too much. It starts at a very young age and creates a lot of bumps in the road for these children.

When an event happens **spur-of-the-moment**, it means that event was not planned in the minds of the Organized Golds. Stress again rears its ugly head. For example, if you need to work late tonight and postpone a planned activity with your Organized Gold child, that can stress them. In addition, if it is a positive spur-of-the-moment idea, they may not respond immediately in the way you had hoped. For example, if you ask them if they would like to go to the store right now for something they want, they may pause, think, and then slowly agree. Momentarily they are stressed by the fact that they are being asked to go on an unplanned activity immediately.

In the minds of the Organized Golds, **change** translates into decreased organization, unfamiliar territory, so to speak. They have their ways of doing things and don't like to change their habits. If, for example, you traditionally go to the cottage or to grandma's house for a holiday weekend, then that is their expectation every year. Their motto would go something like, "If it ain't broke, don't fix it!" The more changes they experience the more stressed they can become. Even something as little as changing plans for a Saturday afternoon can "put them off their game" and be somewhat stressful. Having mom going from a part-time job to a full-time job may affect these children more than you think. They begin to worry about how that will affect life as they have always known it. They may ask questions such as, "Will Mom still be able to pick me up after school? What about getting to my practice; Mom always takes me? Mom always helps me with my projects so what if she is too busy working now?"

Waiting exasperates the Organized Gold unless they planned for it; because clearly if life was perfectly organized there would be no waiting! So waiting for their birthday would be fine because it is something they can plan for yearly. Waiting for a late school bus, however, means someone or something (e.g., bad traffic) messed up the schedule, and they feel stressed. Also, when it comes to making a decision they don't want to wait a long time, once the decision has been made. For example, if they are given the option of going skating, going biking or going to the store in an hour, once Organized Golds make their choice they will be stressed if you don't leave in an hour.

In the Organized Golds' world **emergencies** may be expressed as disorganization. There would not be an emergency if everything went as planned. Emergencies mean the plan is disrupted, or even worse for Organized Golds, there never was a plan. Telling Organized Gold teens that you have an emergency at work, which means you cannot pick them up after school and that they have to find their own ride home can be a real stressor since that disrupts the normal flow of events.

Conflict in relationships spells lack of organization within those relationships for the Organized Golds. Remember these children often grow up to take on the caretaker role both at home and in society, so they will feel stressed even at a young age when faced with conflicting relations. Hearing stories of feuding family members, or having friends at school not getting along can be overwhelming for them. It means the family, or the friendship is not running smoothly any longer.

Linda Berens[5] adds abandonment as a stressor to Organized Golds. Any type of abandonment spells out lack of organization. For example, having to abandon a carefully prepared plan of action, or having a school friend go on vacation, or a teacher leave in the middle of a school year could all be classified as "abandonment" for Organized Golds. As a parent you may not define any of these in the true sense of abandonment, but your Organized Gold child may.

It may surprise you to know that **vacations** for the Organized Golds can stress them out if they are not organized and planned carefully. Daily routines are generally not followed on vacations. One parent told us that he didn't understand that taking a week in the middle of the school term for vacation stresses older Organized Gold children who may worry that they won't get school assignments done; they may also feel responsible for not getting part-time work duties done. Since disruptions in general act as stressors for this dimension, vacations can be considered a stress.

Surprise parties may also upset some Organized Gold kids. Again, this is an event that is not scheduled in their life, so, for them it is disorganized to have a party suddenly happen, even when it is for them! In the case of older Organized Gold children they may feel they are not dressed properly for the party. They may not see a friend in attendance who they would have wanted to come. They may have things they feel they should be doing at this particular moment. The younger child may just burst into tears and you wonder what happened!

Smoothing Out the "Bumps" for Organized Golds' Stress

How can Organized Golds manage over-commitment? They need to know that they can **ask for help**, and do not have to be stoic in doing everything on their own. When you give them permission to ask you, or their teachers, and later, their bosses for help, it is a way of letting them know that they don't always have to work independently of others. One of our granddaughters, who was very independent as a preschooler was known to say, "A little help please!" when she could not tie her shoes or reach a high coat hook. Since then we've often suggested that teaching your Organized Golds at a young age that it is okay to say, "A little help please" to help prevent some future stress.

Organized Golds find it difficult sometimes to **say NO** to taking on responsibilities. Older children especially may join many extracurricular activities and be asked to take a leading role in them. A simple "no" to taking on extra responsibility is something they need to be taught. You could suggest that they join a club, but not become the President of the club, for example. Or they may join a few team sports of their choice, just not all three sports at one time!

Change happens and the Organized Golds need to learn that everything does not remain static. Having said that, however, giving them a little lead time and information to understand the necessity of the change can go a long way to having them "on board" with the change and prevent a lot of their stress. For example, if there will be a change in their mother's work status, as described in the bumps section, let them know what will remain the same to alleviate the initial anxiety and then work slowly into the changes they may have to accept. Even spur-of-the-moment changes can be accepted if you can possibly give them a little lead time (half an hour maybe?)

rather than springing it on them. For example, if your child is working on a new Lego® design give a 10-minute warning that the whole family is going out for an hour or so. They can finish then by putting a few more Lego® pieces in place to ensure that it will be intact upon returning.

While waiting isn't fun for most people, it does cause Organized Golds undue stress because the time feels wasted; yet they need to learn that invariably there will be times they need to **fill in the time** while waiting. Ask them how they can use that time. Have them logically figure out what they might do while waiting for the school bus, or waiting to go somewhere; they may play a game on a device, or the younger ones may play "I spy" with friends while waiting for the school bus. At home, they might read a book, play a game, etc.

In the case of conflict, or "abandonment" as mentioned in the "bumps" section, they may or may not be able to do anything about it. Sometimes they have to learn that they need to find ways that help them to **relax** when something is out of their control. Some programs for youngsters now teach them to count to 8 to calm themselves, or to take 10 deep breaths. Some yoga studios teach youngsters yoga and meditation. These are all good relaxation tools that can help Organized Golds to remain calm.

To eliminate as many emergencies as you can in the life of Organized Golds it would help if you had a backup plan for situations that you know may arise. For example, if you usually pick them up from school you might want to think in terms of a **Plan B** and tell them about it **BEFORE** the emergency arises. **Plan B** could simply be a relative or a trusting friend may have to pinch-hit for you. In our case, our children could walk home, although it was a long walk. They walked the same route home so if we were just a little delayed we could pick them up en route.

In the case of vacations, have Organized Golds help with the planning, so they have some idea of what to expect. They will then feel they have a say in how the routines will be broken and can look forward to the prospect of enjoying some of the new routines they put in place. For example, it might mean they get to sleep in an extra hour every morning because they stay up later at night to do some fun activities. They may not have all of their usual family meals but can look forward to some meals they help plan, perhaps at restaurants they help choose. Older Organized Golds can ask teachers for work they may need to complete while away and most organizations will give part-time students time off if given enough lead time.

As parents you may want to forget about planning surprise parties for your Organized Golds. Instead, like the vacations, let them in on planning their party! Let your kid tell you who they want to invite, when they want it, and what they might like to do. For them the fun is truly in the organizing, not having "surprise" shouted at them. In the case of knowing there will be a surprise party thrown for them by friends, you might want to at least give them a hint that something is up so they can plan to be surprised.

GPS for BUMPS in the Authentic Blues' Journey

Radar Detection for Authentic Blues' Stress

How do you detect the presence of stress in Authentic Blue children? What does distress look like for them? Usually they want to please everyone, build relationships through cooperation and have a positive attitude about life as creative and imaginative thinkers. However, you may encounter the opposite on a less-than-perfect day for your Authentic Blues!

These usually communicative children will **withdraw** and become quieter, more remote, or "zone out." For example, they may come home from school and go straight to their room without saying much of anything. If you ask them about their day they may just shrug their shoulders. At first you may just think they are "out of sorts" but if it continues they are likely stressed about something.

If the stress escalates then they may have **strong emotional outbursts** where they yell and scream. For example, their young sibling, whom they usually get along with quite well, says something innocuous to them at the dinner table and the Authentic Blue lets loose, yelling at the sibling about bugging them all the time.

Sometimes Authentic Blues display their stress by becoming **hyper-critical** about others or even themselves, picking at their own flaws. They may say things like, "I am just no good at math. I cannot do the work. I know I will fail the test. I am never going to understand this theory!" They may point a finger at their best friend, for example, saying something like, "She is a terrible friend who never listens to me!"

Oftentimes Authentic Blues will agree to do something. But when they say **"Yes" and then don't follow through** it can be a sign that they are stressed. For example, in the morning you asked your child to start dinner, giving easy instructions. She agreed to do so. But when you get home late from work, nothing has been started; the oven isn't even turned on!

When Authentic Blues **act out to get your attention** they are stressed. Generally they are helpful and cooperative, but when they misbehave purposely then something is very wrong. Young children may hit or bite a younger sibling to get your attention. Older children may refuse to play with their younger siblings when usually they are happy to do so. Teens may not take the dog out for a walk after school, despite knowing that the poor thing needs to relieve itself, and you will notice!

If stress continues to build then the usually-pleasant, helpful Authentic Blues may start **making excuses** for not doing something that they normally are happy to do. For example, you may ask them to water the plants in the garden, but now they tell you they don't have time, they have to go to their friend's after school, etc. This is a clue that something, besides plant watering, may be bothering them.

Finally, **physically** the stressed out Authentic Blue may **crave more** food or eat more snacks. Even though there have been large meals at dinner time, you may recognize that for the last little while that your child just can't seem to get filled up. They overeat every evening, which is something they don't usually do.

"Bumps" Encountered in the Authentic Blues' Journey

Here's a little reminder. The Authentic Blues' core needs include feeling better and better about themselves every day and having harmonious relationships. Some values include enthusiasm, approval, being with others and encouragement.

Often when you turn the good things upside down and have a look at what happens when the day doesn't go well; you'll soon recognize the stressors in your Authentic Blues' lives, at least from the point of view of their natures.

If you think about the word AUTHENTIC as the descriptor for Blues, then anything that is "un-authentic" acts as a stressor for this group. Let's see what we mean...

Authentic Blues desire harmony in their lives and when there is any kind of **conflict** they feel stressed. The conflict may not involve them directly, but it may be between their family members or their friends or their part-time job co-workers. It could be an ongoing conflict in the classroom that upsets their school day. Their stress level begins to rise when there is even the hint of an ensuing conflict. If their siblings are raising their voices, they will begin to cringe with the stress.

Being in an **environment** that does not have a harmonious "vibe" will stress this colour. It may be an impersonal atmosphere at a friend's house that they find stressful, so they may ask whether the friend can always come to their house due to their uneasiness at the friend's. Or it might be a hostile environment that they intuitively pick up on and they do not want to stay. They may feel hostility amongst co-workers in a part-time job, although nothing may actually be said. One parent told us that as a teen she babysat for a family of three children. She now understood her uneasiness in their home was probably due to the fact that she "picked up" the disharmony between the parents in her various conversations with them and described their home as not having a good "vibe."

Guilt creates a lot of stress for this dimension — they want to please everyone in their lives. In parent seminars, for example, when guilt is mentioned as a stressor, Authentic Blue adults nod their heads in agreement and often confess to having difficulty with guilt themselves. It can begin at a very young age if Authentic Blues feel that they have not pleased their parents, their teachers, and/or their friends. For example, they may feel guilty if they have not had time to finish the tasks assigned at home. They may feel guilty if their parents won't allow them to go to a friend's house after school when they had promised the friend they would come over. Or they feel guilty if they get into a fight with their siblings, even if the siblings started the fight!

They want authentic people in their lives. They are stressed by **insincere, dishonest or exploitive people**. If they have friends who tell fibs, or little "white lies" they feel very stressed around them. If they have a friend who appears to be their "best friend" but then says something behind their back they may be so stressed that they won't be friends with that insincere person anymore. They can become extremely stressed by stories of people who are unfair or even exploitive of others, which is the reason that the Authentic Blues will often take on social justice and environmental causes.

Routines, repetition and mindless work stress these creative idealists. The youngsters want to please their parents by making their beds, and tidying up their rooms every day. However, they dislike the routine, repetitious, mindless work of doing it on a daily basis. They may dislike a subject at school that requires them to learn by rote since once again they find the repetition somewhat agonizing.

Conformity can be stressful for this dimension. They are generally creatively individualistic in their approach to their lives. For example, Authentic Blues may not like wearing a uniform to school. They may be stressed if you insist on making them conform to your standards, whether it is about hair, clothes, or even studying.

Broken promises stress this dimension a lot since they themselves are authentic and believe everyone should keep their promises. For example, if you promise that you will take them to a friend's cottage next Saturday and then find something prevents you from doing so, your Authentic Blues will view that as a broken promise and be stressed.

Something we hear over and over from Authentic Blue parents is the stress of **evaluations, criticisms** and the worst, **rejection**. Even if they are the people giving the evaluation and the criticism! If you have Authentic Blue children consider yourself forewarned that tests and report cards can be very stressful for them, even if they are "A" students! And if they are teens who are dating, then rejection can lead to a great deal of stress too

Smoothing Out the "Bumps" for Authentic Blues' Stress

When it comes to conflict Authentic Blues may not be able to express their feelings of stress to those they are directly involved with, such as their siblings or other family members. Oftentimes they may have to realize that they cannot stop the conflict happening between other people. Hostile environments may be difficult to do much about either, especially if it is at a friend's home. To reduce some of their own stress over these issues they may have to learn to "let it go" through **self care**. Help them to understand that to live a meaningful, purpose-filled life they need to discover what works to maintain their physical and emotional health. Introduce them to a variety of options such as yoga, running, controlled breathing and/or meditation.

Teach your Authentic Blue children that **guilt is a trap**. Youngsters need to understand that more often than not the people they think they have offended think nothing of it. For example, the friend in the above "bumps" section knows that the Authentic Blue will be allowed to come over another day. The siblings may be using the knowledge that the Authentic Blue feels guilty easily; recognizing this will set the Authentic Blues free of self-defeating behaviour throughout their childhood. They need to know that they can and must take control of their thoughts and stop themselves from going over and over the episode in their heads.

Being authentic themselves and setting their own **priorities** will help Authentic Blues create more relationships with people that will prove to be empowering and ultimately cause them less stress. Hand-in-hand with setting priorities is learning to use the word "no" when it comes to working and playing with others. They need to decide what and who are high on their list of importance and remain steadfast in their decisions.

Have them design ways to be **creative** when it comes to routines, rote studying or repetition. Have them think about how they can mix up the routines and still get the job done. Maybe you can help them by suggesting alternating the order in which they do their chores. Make it fun. They like concepts and new theories. For example, tell them they can boost their brain power by brushing their teeth with their alternate hand, according to a recent study. Going over and over fractions gets monotonous for some Authentic Blues, so bake a real pie and have them cut it up into halves, quarters, thirds, etc. Then you can all have dessert! Create silly songs or find them on the Internet (e.g., the periodic table of elements on YouTube); that helps them with rote learning. We read Dennis Lee's *Alligator Pie*[6] to our own kids and they remembered all of the Canadian towns named in the poem for years afterwards.

While they may have to understand that there are times and places where they may need to conform throughout their lives, teach your Authentic Blues that there also may be room for some **latitude** and that being a non-conformist has its place too. For example, conforming to a school uniform code may be a necessity. However, giving them some latitude and choice in their street clothes can go a long way to de-stressing the Authentic Blues. Our own children wore a school uniform but were allowed to choose their other clothes.

As for broken promises, they may as well know that this will happen from time to time. They need to **learn to calm down**, perhaps with some of the self care tools suggested above. Then they can ask what happened. In many cases there is a perfectly good reason. In the example above, perhaps the car needs repair or the weather is not conducive to driving to a cottage. You might also want to re-think promising them 100% that you will do something. Change it to something like, "We will see what Saturday brings; we may go to your friend's cottage for the day." As one mother of an Authentic Blue told me, "They need to forgive and carry on with their day!"

You can help them to understand that evaluation and criticism can be good and that they can learn from them. Help them learn to **judge the criticism** before judging themselves and getting stressed. Did it come from a teacher who is helping them become a better person? Or did it come from a friend and was said in a mean-spirited way? If from the teacher, then Authentic Blues can learn from it; if from the angry friend then they need to once again "let it go" and realize that it is not worth their time to ponder it, never mind be stressed by it. Help them understand that rejection is difficult for everyone and unfortunately is a part of life. They need to know that while it does not feel good to be rejected by someone, they cannot let others take away their happiness and cause them stress. Help them be resilient and bounce back from rejection in order to move forward.

GPS for BUMPS in the Resourceful Oranges' Journey

Radar Detection for Resourceful Oranges' Stress

How do you detect the presence of stress in Resourceful Orange children? What does distress look like for them? They usually don't take life too seriously, and in fact, are mostly looking for fun and adventure. They seem to handle stress better than the other dimensions, however, they too can have a stress-filled day; here are your clues...

When these usually fun-loving children become **rude and confrontational** you know they are stressed about something! A sibling might need the computer which they share, to do some research. It might be a common request but this time the Resourceful Orange becomes confrontational saying something like, "Well I'm using it now so you cannot have it!" They may also lash out boisterously at someone. For example, you may ask them casually how they are doing with their homework or a project. They reply with, "You are always on my case. Why can't you just for once leave me alone?"

Some Resourceful Oranges may go even further and get **physically aggressive**. This occurs when they are at their boiling point and will fight back. They may actually hit, kick or punch their friend, their sibling or you. This behaviour is not acceptable, of course, but it is a clue that something is definitely stressing them out!

They may even **run away**. These children don't like sitting still at the best of times. They are usually physically active. So when they are particularly stressed by something at home or school they may decide to run away. Hopefully they do not get far before you realize they are gone and begin contacting their friends! The distance they get naturally depends on their age — the younger they are, the closer to home they will probably be found.

They don't normally appreciate rules but when they purposely and blatantly **break the rules** then you can tell they are stressed. For example, an older child whose job it is to start dinner chooses not to do so. They may also take risks along with breaking the rules, such as not coming home after their practice as they always do, or choosing to go out with their older friends without asking your permission.

Another stress clue for Resourceful Oranges is that of not quite telling the truth or **misrepresenting the truth**. For example, your child comes home with an "F" on a test. You say, "I thought you told me you had studied for that test. What happened?" The Resourceful Oranges now confess that they forgot their books at school the night before so had not actually studied, ending with, "But it's not my fault!"

If you see that they are **procrastinating** about getting something done it may be another stress clue. Usually they get their work done as quickly as possible so that they can get on with things they like to do. This doesn't mean they are sitting still; they are likely keeping themselves busy doing something active and may be seen as "clowning around." This clue may be a little more difficult to perceive since it doesn't "look" like stress.

Physical symptoms can sometimes be the easiest to spot, although this dimension doesn't usually suffer from them as much as the others. In the case of the Resourceful Oranges, they may have decreased appetites so you will observe a change in their eating pattern. They may also suffer some memory loss, which is also easy to spot. They may forget to go to practice — something they never want to skip!

"Bumps" Encountered in the Resourceful Oranges' Journey

Resourceful Oranges need to feel they have some freedom with a lot of variety and activity thrown in for good measure. Some of their values include creative freedom, performance, trying new things, little supervision and having skills noticed.

Now that you have the clues and your radar is ready, you can watch for the dimension stressors that make their day a little less than happy.

RESOURCEFUL describes this dimension, so if they cannot use their creativity in a resourceful way they will feel stressed. Here are some stressors for this group...

Rigid rules can make this normally fun-loving personality stressed because there is no room for freedom of expression, or freedom to do! If you are a parent who feels that a number of specific rules must be enforced to make a home run smoothly, then expect a lot of stress on the part of your freedom-loving kid. One parent told us, "I just don't get why there was so much push back from my Resourceful Orange child." Once she listed all the rules of her household though, we understood!

Constant **routine** creates stress for this personality dimension. They want to hurry up and get things done that need to be done so they can get on with the "fun stuff" of life. Routine is just not fun for them. Doing the same things every day or every weekend becomes boring (we called it the "b" word in our house). For example, having to practice piano every day at four o'clock becomes irritating for them, no matter how much they like to play.

Micromanaging this dimension usually contributes to their stress. Standing over them, ensuring that everything gets done, or sending texts to make sure they are getting their chores done serves only to make them work less and stress more. One father told us, "I had to check every five minutes to make sure my child was getting the assigned chores done, or else that kid would be off somewhere else." When we asked if his child got the work done he said, "It gets done with a lot of frustration on the part of both of us." He also added, "Raising kids is just exhausting!"

Sitting in one place being still is a hardship for these active people. Being told to sit at a table until something is done can be agonizing for them. One Resourceful Orange parent indicated that he still has trouble sitting for any length of time at work, or at home and that he is generally on the move every so often.

For this dimension anything with **abstract concepts** can be stressful unless it can be made relevant to what they need to do. They are more tactile, hands-on in their approach. Going into all the abstract reasons why they should do something does nothing but make them stressed. One parent, who happens to be a psychologist, told us that her bright Resourceful Orange just throws their hands up if she starts talking psychological theory to make a point!

Has your Resourceful Orange child told you that they sometimes feel **taken for granted** when they feel that their family members and friends should have been impressed with their actions? Naturally this stresses them out. Because they enjoy life and don't stress easily, other colours may have a tendency to take them for granted. One parent told us that he realized he kept chastising his Resourceful Orange offspring for not putting the tools away correctly after the same child had spent an entire afternoon helping him fix their fence after a wind storm. One mom realized that her Resourceful Orange child often makes the popcorn for movie night, and desserts on the weekend with little appreciation from the other family members.

Tom Maddron[7] indicates that Resourceful Oranges get stressed if there is **no challenge** for them. These adventurous risk-takers find life without a challenge somewhat stressful because there is nothing to strive towards. For example, some parents are so "hands-on" that they want to keep their child from being too challenged, or perhaps they don't want to see them hurt by doing something like trying out for the regionals in sports because they may not get chosen. This may backfire with Resourceful Oranges who become stressed from a lack of challenges!

On the other hand, giving the Resourceful Oranges **a lot of responsibility** can also be stressful for them. So while they want some challenge, they don't want to take on more than they feel they want to handle. Be careful as parents thinking that because your children are at a certain age they can handle the same responsibilities that you did when you were their age. Your offspring may be able to walk the dog after school, but it may be too much to expect them to babysit younger siblings as well.

Smoothing Out the "Bumps" for Resourceful Oranges' Stress

Relaxing the rules at home can go a long way to decreasing your child's stress, especially if they have to bear more rules than they want to at school or in extracurricular activities. You may have to prioritize the rules that need to be kept, and loosen your hold on some of the others. For example, one parent did not allow her children to ever go to a friend's house on a school night but found that her children did their homework faster and without complaint when they were allowed a little latitude with that rule. With the rules you do have, be consistent. Make promises rather than threats. Otherwise, breaking the rule becomes a fun challenge.

Let your Resourceful Oranges have a little **flexibility and creativity** when it comes to routine. Perhaps you have to get the groceries done on the weekend with your kids in tow but throw in a fun trip to the toy store on the way home. Or maybe you could do errands while your preteen is at a friend's house so they don't always have to go on routine trips with you.

Stop micromanaging; let your kids know that you will reduce your overseeing if they can prove to you that they can get their work done without constant intervention by you. Their stress level will decrease and there is a good chance that they will get the work done faster and more efficiently. Let them know that they should ask for help whenever they get "stuck."

Avoid making them sit still in one place too long. When they start fidgeting have something **physical** they can do or let them use their own resourcefulness to figure out something they can do for a few minutes. These children usually have so much energy that they could burst if they have to sit long. So let them "get physical." Before, during and after they have to sit for awhile let them jump rope, do jumping jacks, play outside, or just play with play-dough, etc. We have a mini trampoline in our house that all of the grandchildren invariably jump on when they visit; it's just fun!

Let them **"catch" abstract concepts** in a fun creative way. Adult Resourceful Oranges tell us that they can focus better when their eyes and hands are busy. Have you ever watched someone knitting while they carried on a conversation? It's as though the fidgety side of the brain needs a little entertainment while the reasoning side can take in the information. Let them put Lego together while you explain a concept to them. Or play catch with them if you want to ask them multiplication tables. Make it a game and they will be de-stressed!!

Take time to appreciate the things that the Resourceful Oranges do. Don't get caught up in what they should do or could be. If, for example, they spend time fixing the fence with you, tell them you appreciate their help rather than complaining because they didn't put a tool away. If they make the popcorn or special desserts, let them know that it is wonderful! We have parents tell us that they don't think their appreciate them but then they realize that they themselves don't always let their Resourceful Oranges (and other children for that matter) know how much they are appreciated either.

Tom Maddron makes the bold statement that Resourceful Oranges "thrive on **challenge**... and on reaching for new heights of performance."[8] Have you ever noticed how Olympic athletes will often attribute their own success to their parents and/or a great coach who both supported and challenged them to perform better and better. When you see something your child is good at, challenge them to improve. This is what they will remember in the long run! For example, if they run a 10-kilometre race, encourage them to enter the half marathon next, if that is what they want to do!

Listen carefully to Resourceful Oranges so you know when you can add to their **responsibilities** at home. Remember, this is about your child's journey, rather than your journey as a child; the two could be very different. So if you were able to walk the dog, take care of your siblings, and get your homework done before dinner that is wonderful. Your Resourceful Oranges may not be ready for all the responsibility. Try one thing at a time and then start adding. It is also helpful if it relates to their interests in any way. For example, when we both worked full time away from home our Resourceful Orange made dinner every evening. It was a big responsibility that she handled beautifully by 16; something we had started and encouraged when she was much younger by having her stir the cookie dough.

GPS for BUMPS in the Inquiring Greens' Journey

Radar Detection for Inquiring Greens' Stress

How do you detect the presence of stress in Inquiring Green children? What does distress look like for them? Since they generally are not overly expressive and are somewhat independent, it may be difficult to know when these somewhat serious children are feeling stressed. Here are the signs to watch for that tell you when Inquiring Greens are experiencing a less-than-perfect day.

When your Inquiring Green children display **impatience, frustration** and a **"short fuse"** this may indicate stress. Maybe they cannot move up a level in one of their games or they just cannot build the Lego figure the way they had planned. Or they checked their school marks to find they did not achieve their own high standard.

Their stress may go up a notch if they become very angry, **enraged** and/or blow up. We have observed this ourselves with an Inquiring Green who is great with all the devices you can buy, but becomes explosive when those devices don't work properly!

On the other hand, the Inquiring Green may exhibit **extreme aloofness and withdrawal**. It might be difficult to spot immediately since Inquiring Greens are generally quiet and independent anyway. So keep your radar ready for the more extreme situations when they might be stressed. Perhaps they are feeling incompetent because they don't understand a new concept or theory to their satisfaction.

They may display a **cool, unfeeling exterior** and appear to be **insensitive** too. If they usually interact with siblings or friends in a warm, friendly way then there may be something that is stressing them. Perhaps someone has hurt their feelings and they are responding by being insensitive to others.

They may also start making **sarcastic remarks** or even appear to be quite arrogant around family members. As they get into preteen and teen years peer pressure builds and this may be the way your Inquiring Green handles it, especially if their wisecracks get a laugh or two from their peers!

Inquiring Greens display stress when they become very **critical**, of themselves and/or others. Often if they have expressed their feelings openly or blown up they may turn to criticism, because they are angry at themselves for making such a display. They like to be cool, calm and collected.

This colour may have physical symptoms of stress as a result of feeling pressured on the inside. They may have stomach aches, headaches or even back pain for seemingly no apparent reason.

"Bumps" Encountered in the Inquiring Greens' Journey

Happiness for Inquiring Greens includes feeling they are knowledgeable and competent. These children value their independence and their abstract thinking. They like to discover things on their own and appreciate progress. Some values include intelligence, freedom to ask questions, high standards and private thinking time.

Your radar may be telling you that your Inquiring Greens are feeling stressed. Let's look at some of the stressors they may be dealing with at this time.

INQUIRING describes this dimension; if they cannot use their competence to satisfy their curiosity they may feel stressed. Here are some stressors for this group.

A display of **emotions** can be very stressful for Inquiring Greens who generally feel more comfortable with facts, ideas and data. Furthermore, they are frustrated if people don't think they have emotions; they just don't choose to express them often. For example, if a sibling or a friend bursts into tears they may get too stressed or flustered to know what to do for that friend or sibling.

Tom Maddron tells us that "the everyday social world can be a real nuisance for (Inquiring) Greens."[9] If they have to socialize too much, and this is not comfortable for them, then it may not just be a nuisance, but a stressor. One main reason revolves around the notion that they want to talk at length about what interests them with one or two people, but that can be difficult since others often focus on **small talk**, for which Inquiring Greens have little use.

When Inquiring Greens feel incompetent they are stressed. If they are playing a game on the Internet or with a friend they may become very stressed when not winning. They may receive a poor grade — or what they consider a poor grade — on a test or a report card, and that stresses them considerably. They may strive for perfection and find that they just cannot attain such a high standard, which perplexes them even more.

These children like to be in control of their own lives. They are stressed if you are too controlling — telling them what to do and when to do it, resulting in a **lack of independence**. They don't want to have to depend on anyone for anything. Parents of Inquiring Greens will think back to when these children were preschoolers, insisting that they could dress themselves and being stressed when it took too long! As teens they may get stressed because they want to work alone in a part-time job only to find that there are too many co-workers in their space.

Routines stress Inquiring Greens because they get in the way of discovering new and important things that they find interesting. They will ask point blank, "What use is it to make my bed if I am just going to climb back into it tonight?" One parent acknowledged that while his wife routinely had her hair cut every six weeks he has always found it stressful to have to get his hair cut on such a regular basis because it might take him away from doing something much more interesting!

Repetition and redundancy stress Inquiring Greens, because, according to Tom Maddron, it might imply "that I am stupid by telling me something a second time."[10] In their case repetition and redundancy is not so much about being bored, as in the case of the Resourceful Oranges; it is more about not wanting to be perceived as lacking in competence.

Inquiring Greens find **inflexibility** very difficult to handle. They want the flexibility to research, discover and think things through for themselves. When they are dealing with a parent, a friend, or a teacher who wants it done their way and their way only, Inquiring Greens get stressed. There may be another way that could even be better. Ironically, **too many details** can act as a stressor for the Inquiring

Greens! Considering that they are the people who like to read, do research and discover new materials, it is surprising that they can have too many details swirling around in their brain. Temperament theorists refer to it as "analysis paralysis." For example, one dad told us about his Inquiring Green child who, as a youngster, took apart many things at once, would then look at all the parts, analyze them, yet not seem to be able to figure out how to put the items back together again properly. Dad went on to say, "It was as if there were just too many parts."

Smoothing Out the "Bumps" for Inquiring Greens' Stress

Inquiring Greens would prefer it if you expressed yourself **logically** using **facts and data**, rather than emotions. They enjoy debate and will even engage in confrontation rather than display much emotion. It is much better to use a calm, reassuring voice with them.

Although some Inquiring Greens may prefer to be by themselves, (especially Introverts!) exploring their own interests, they do need to be able to function in **social settings**. Encourage them to have their friends over to do things together such as building a Lego structure, or, when they are older, going hiking with more than one friend at a time. Providing them with a few social graces can help them in social situations as well. For example, teach them to greet guests who come to visit; and eat together as a family, when possible, to help socialize your Inquiring Greens. Other Inquiring Greens are very comfortable with, and may seek the company of, others so this isn't a concern.

Learning to **accept** that they may not be perfect or competent in everything that they attempt will go a long way toward helping decrease their stress for the rest of their lives. Teaching them that doing their best sometimes means getting a "B" rather than an "A" is what is important. This is not an easy lesson for them to learn but it will serve them well if they can learn to say something like, "I did the best that I could!"

Being in complete control, independent of others, is not something to strive for all the time. Inquiring Greens need to grasp that learning to share and being interdependent can be beneficial since they will likely have to work in groups at school and in the workforce. You can help them by keeping them **connected** and interactive with siblings and friends.

It is helpful if you can have Inquiring Greens understand that some routines make the day run smoothly. However, that being said, taking away what Tom Maddron refers to as "nonsense schedules"[11] can go a long way to de-stressing your Inquiring Greens. In other words, "less is more" when it comes to routines for these children. Keeping the **routines to a bare minimum** will allow them to see the logic behind having to get up, go to school, shower and go to bed in order to be successful human beings. Perhaps a little latitude in the exact time they need to arise or go to bed would be helpful. Perhaps not having to shower every night at the exact time would help. Let them have some control and independence in setting some of their routines, especially as they become teenagers. Be sure to give them a rationale for a rule or routine so they can reason it out for themselves.

Telling Inquiring Greens something repeatedly seems like nagging to them. Stop doing it. They usually do "get it" the first time you tell them and it saves them from appearing to be incompetent. Try saying something once and see if they understand. Or say it and then ask, "Do you have any questions?" Chances are they will question something, but that can lead into a discussion rather than a nagging session.

Providing Inquiring Greens with more **flexibility** helps decrease their frustration. They like to think for themselves. Having everything dictated to them in an inflexible manner will only serve to make them angry, frustrated people. Let them strategize with you to get everything done that they need to rather than tell them when and how things will be accomplished. If they have chores to do, be flexible about when they need to be done. Asking them to figure out how to put the garbage out in time for the garbage pickup, for example, allows them a little flexibility as to when they need to do it. Telling them to do it immediately after dinner sets you up for debate because they see that as being inflexible.

Have a look at their schedule to see if you can free up some time for them so they will feel considerably less stressed. Allow them time to discover, to contemplate, to think about "what if." Refrain from having their every minute scheduled so they can have, **uninterrupted time** to focus on the things that interest them.

To help alleviate the stress that comes with "analysis paralysis" you may want to discuss their projects, or items they took apart (as in the last point in the "bumps" section). That father could help his kids figure out how to **strategize**; it is a way for them to learn how to prioritize. For example, they could start with what items were taken apart and then what parts might go with each item and then where each part might fit.

Now that we have detected stress and have some ways to smooth it out, what about communicating with our kids? Well you guessed it, each personality dimension also has its unique communicating style. Let's see how we can crack that code in the next chapter!

Chapter 6

GPS FOR POSITIVE COMMUNICATION ON YOUR JOURNEY

It will come as no surprise that each personality dimension has its own preferences when it comes to communication. Once we provide you with GPS for communicating with each of the four dimensions we hope you'll have even more successful conversations with your children on your parenting journey!

Communication Style Reflected in Words and Action

When it comes to words and action (or "saying" and "doing"), it is easier to spot in children than in adults[1], because kids are pretty open. Their words and actions that they use reflect their communication style. And, you guessed it, the four innate groups have different combinations resulting in four different communication styles.[2]

Words revolve around one of two questions: "What is?" or "What's possible?" Children who tend to talk about "What is" make observations based on their five senses; their words will be concrete, practical and descriptive. For example, one Grade 8 student observed a picture of a woman at Boston's Gardner Museum: "I think this woman is a queen because she has a crown on. She's dressed very fancy. She is staring at something we can't see. Her left hand is in a pose that looks like she dropped something. She has a gold circle ..."[3]

Children who like to talk about "What's possible" focus on imagination using their sixth sense to imagine, to think, to believe things, describing more abstract concepts. For example, another Grade 8 student describes the picture of a chair at the Gardner Museum: "If I could take anything in the gallery, I would take one of the bright red chairs that drip with the essence of royalty. These chairs seem to be straight from the imagery of a dream in which one becomes a king or queen and is seated in a chair like this."[4]

Action revolves around one of two questions: "What works" or "What's right." Children who tend to do "what works" set out to succeed in getting what they want, no matter what their parents or other adults may say, such as "be good" or "behave!"

On the other hand, those children who tend to do "what's right" generally set out to get what they want, while at the same time respecting the rules and pleasing parents and other adults, preferring not to question authority figures.

Journal Sample: At the end of this section for each personality dimension you will find an excerpt from a Grade 8 student's journal entry. These students were a group of singers/actors who had been chosen to perform in the production of Andrew Lloyd Webber's *Joseph and the Amazing Technicolour Dreamcoat* in Toronto, Canada. Kate was privileged to work with these students who journalled about their respective experiences during the rehearsals. Kate read the journal entries and gave her responses. She subsequently wrote an article, *Journal Writing: A Means to Self-Discovery*, which was then published under the name Darlene E. Jones.[5]

Radar Detection

Your **radar** can detect a personality dimension through body movement, appearance and even demeanor. We will give you some clues to observe in each of the four dimensions.[6]

Let's take a look at each personality dimension, with a little help, once again, from some Disney characters, to understand whether their **words** focus on "what is" or "what's possible" and if their **action** is based on "what works" or "what's right," and then finally explore clues with our **radar**.

GPS for Organized Golds' Communication Style

"Just as I thought — Mary Poppins, practically perfect in every way."[7]
~Mary Poppins

Mary Poppins, a beloved Disney classic, inspired Walt Disney Studios to create Saving Mr. Banks, a movie based on how they made Mary Poppins! When our granddaughter met Mary Poppins at Walt Disney World® Magic Kingdom® Theme Park her eyes were as big as saucers and she could only nod in response to Mary's questions! It was a very hot day but Mary Poppins still had her hair perfectly coiffed and her button-up shirt perfectly starched to accentuate the commanding way of the Banks' nanny. Mary Poppins is representative of Organized Golds, so let's find out what it is about their communication style that we see in Mary Poppins...

Some real people who may exemplify this communication style, according to David Keirsey, include some corporate CEOs, military officers and some high ranking politicians, specifically President Truman.[8] Other examples? What about Berkshire Hathaway CEO

Warren Buffet, Queen Elizabeth II, and journalist Barbara Walters? Let's see why these names may be on the list...

Words and Actions Reflect Communication Style

"What is ..."

Organized Golds are natural observers and so generally use concrete, practical words. They describe **"what is"** using their five senses. They like to discuss "solid and sensible topics."[9] Organized Gold children talk about their collections, hobbies, schedules, sports scores. They tell you exact information about the things that they enjoy. No surprise that the symbol for this group is the check mark because they will list the items they have and those they still want to complete their collection. If they enjoy a subject at school they can tell you specific facts and figures. It is generally concrete data they happily disclose though; asking them abstract questions may cause them to shut down.

Like Mary Poppins, their speaking style is direct and sequential, moving from one topic to the next in a consistent manner. They use simple words, easily understood for the listener. Often they relate topics to themselves such as, "Yesterday, I found out ..." They often focus on specific details, sharing little about their feelings. They may include information about people, places and things. They like to use comparative language, such as "this bike is better than my last one because ...", or "I don't have enough games for my device." They also use the possessive when speaking about their life, saying, "my school," "my team," "my dog," "my class," etc.

They easily handle the normal flow of conversation, using their skill of associating facts that they have retained with the topics at hand. Since they prefer solid, practical facts to abstract ideas they often guide the conversation back to "what is." As an example, they may lead their group by keeping them on track, literally changing a discussion from the team's vision for the finals to the more practical concerns of the current meeting with "so what is the game plan for tomorrow?"

"What's right ... "

This personality dimension usually gets what they want by cooperating and doing **"what's right."** Think of the way Mary Poppins gained the Banks' children's cooperation. Organized Golds are generally comfortable joining groups and attending extended family functions since they are adept in most social settings.

Organized Golds generally like simple, conventional language, preferring the more established and traditionally used words that reflect "what's right" in communities. For example, they may use old proverbs to express a general truth, usually about amount or usefulness, such as: "it pays to be prepared," "learn from your mistakes." They generally pick up on (and will retain for life) the language used by those around them in their home environment, their town, wherever they grow up.

Older Organized Gold children speak to younger children much like Mary Poppins spoke to her charges! They listen to the rules and generally follow them, expecting everyone else to do the same. So, even as youngsters, their language is peppered with warnings, counselling and judgements, such as: "you ought to get your work done or you'll be in trouble," or "be careful crossing the street when the crossing guard isn't there," or "you should keep your room tidier."

Journal Sample: Organized Golds' writing tends to be simple and logical, laced with facts and details. Their journals often have detailed specifics outlining the day's events, like a checklist. For example, in Kate's article on journal writing, Shenelle writes facts with a little admonishment at the end: "She's nice. She speaks with a British accent and she's pregnant. Now my mom had a baby three months ago and I always read the pregnancy book. Now tell me if I'm wrong but pregnant ladies shouldn't be jumping around should they? Well (she) was anyway!"[10]

Your Radar for Organized Gold Communicators

Usually this temperament group does not **gesture** when speaking. David Keirsey[11] tells us that they generally have few hand movements, unless they become very excited or moved about something. Watch for a wagging index finger, while they say something like, "you better not mess my things up again!" If they use a swift chopping motion with one or both hands, they are demonstrating that you better listen because this is very important. For example, if really aggravated by a sibling messing up their space, the motion of chopping tells the younger one, "I mean it this time!" They may also use this chopping motion to emphasize that the discussion is closed, depending on the context of the conversation. Alternatively, some Organized Golds are more expressive non verbally and may use gestures as a way of relating to and connecting with others.

Because they "should," Organized Golds generally stand straight and sit up straight, just like Mary Poppins. This group is very socially aware so they will learn and practice the social norms such as waving hello and goodbye from a very early age, relating to people pleasantly. As they mature, they will very ably and willingly introduce friends to you.

These children care about being suitably dressed without having to attract a lot of attention within their groups. They want their **appearance** to reflect their organized way of life, so they like to present themselves as well groomed overall; Mary Poppins always looked well groomed and proper! They don't usually argue with you about having regular scheduled baths (or showers), teeth brushing and haircuts because they want to take good care of their own bodies. In essence, they want to portray, through their appearance, that they are "someone who is put together."[12]

Organized Golds generally reflect their responsible, serious manner in a consistent clear tone of voice. They usually know and take their rightful place in the home, at school and in groups. They generally follow the rules so are most often the cooperative kids, ready to help you and others on their journey. They enjoy planning and organizing ahead of time and will remain calm and usually cautious in order to make sure they observe the rules and routines of daily living.

As we wave goodbye to Mary Poppins we hope you will continue to enjoy the cooperative spirit of your Organized Golds who, like Mary, observe what needs to be done and then set about to get everyone on board!

GPS for Authentic Blues' Communication Style

"What makes someone special? I suppose it all depends. It's what's unique in each of us."

"Who says that my dreams have to stay just my dreams?"
~Ariel, The Little Mermaid

In Disney's 1989 musical fantasy film, we meet Ariel under the water, since she is a mermaid princess. Somewhat independent, she daydreams a lot and also has fun singing and playing with her best fish friend, Flounder. Despite warnings from her father, the king, and advisor Sebastian, that merpeople and humans are not to have contact, she dreams about marrying a human and becoming a human herself. Our granddaughters remember meeting her in her lagoon, sitting, tail and all, looking quite beautiful. They were thrilled when this real mermaid asked, "Are you humans or mermaids?"

David Keirsey's famous Authentic Blues include Emily Dickinson, William Blake, and Ghandi[13]. Others? We also wonder about Emily Bronte, Dostoevsky, Helen Keller, Mr. (Fred) Rogers, Princess Diana, Carl Rogers, Martin Luther King Jr., and Dr. Seuss? Let's see why these names may very well be on the list...

Words and Actions Reflect Communication Style

"What's possible ..."

Authentic Blue children naturally lean towards their "vivid imagination and sense of fantasy"[14] when thinking and so their words are abstract, full of **"what's possible."** While they may observe real things they choose to discuss their inner world of thoughts, spiritual beliefs and personal insights. Like Ariel they want to dream of something beyond the world they currently live in, the day-to-day practicalities. Ariel wanted to join the world of the humans; your Authentic Blue children will be inspired by their own dreams, fantasies, and ideals. Their language often focuses on character, personalities, love, hate, heart, soul, stories, legends, fairy tales and, of course, possibilities.

To come up with "what's possible" Authentic Blues may make intuitive leaps in their thoughts, often reading between the lines to interpret what is being hinted at, suggested or unseen. They disclose hunches and personal interpretations of a situation or another's comments or actions. In other words, they often infer general laws from one particular instance. For example, Ariel concludes that it would be better to be a human than a mermaid from having watched one human!

Authentic Blues try to make you understand what they are thinking through a variety of ways. They will often use metaphors, and probably would like these: the recess bell was music to my ears; you are my sunshine; life is just a bowl of cherries; and the eyes are the windows of the soul.[15]

They use analogies to show you how two things that are different from one another have something in common. Examples may include common sayings such as, you're as quiet as a mouse; the paint was as blue as the ocean; the baby was as cute as a button; my love is as deep as the ocean.

Or they will use their own experiences to get a point across. For example they might like relating how they overcame their fear of dogs by going to a dog show at the Winter Fair.

These usually articulate children usually speak openly about their emotions unless they don't feel safe in doing so. They may cry as they tell you how sad they are about a story heard at school. Older children will resonate with certain poets who move them emotionally to exclaim "how beautiful," or "how sad," or "how inspiring!" Quotes they may like include: Dickinson's "Hope is the thing with feathers that perches in the soul — and sings the tunes without the words — and never stops at all."[16] Or Rumi's "You were born with wings, why prefer to crawl through life?"[17]

A dead give-away that you are talking to an Authentic Blue is their use of universal language, often in a theatrical way. They tend to overstate the situation or the experience, saying something like, *"You NEVER let me do anything!"* or *"Why do I ALWAYS have to be the first one to come home?"* If they are telling you about a new subject, they may say it is *"UTTERLY revolting,"* or alternatively, *"it is ABSOLUTELY exciting."*

"What's right ..."

Authentic Blues often get excited when speaking. Like Organized Golds, this dimension usually gets what they want by cooperating and doing **"what's right."** After all, their symbol is one of hands joined together. They get quite animated in order to make sure that you understand what it is they are telling you.

They dream of a perfect world that is at peace, with everyone enjoying perfect relationships and supportive interactions. They want to relate to people in a personal way, to ensure enduring relationships. They like to impress their listeners, inspire them, and influence them in a positive way. These children often grow up to be therapists, counsellors, primary school teachers or motivational speakers, etc. They sometimes provide you with a hint of this calling in their choice of words, such as, "You won't believe it; this is AMAZING!" Or if you do something for them they may say, "You are WONDERFUL!"

Journal Sample: In terms of writing, Authentic Blues' journals are filled with descriptions of their feelings and imaginative thoughts. An excerpt from Kate's article by Allecia, who initially didn't feel like writing, but does the assignment anyway to please and then wrote feverishly for pages: "To Mrs. J: You might have noticed I've written a lot more than I usually do. I read over the papers that you gave us and then made a mental vow to try to write more whenever I have time. I really didn't feel like writing today but I tried to write one paragraph and my pen took over!" She wrote four full pages of narrative, interspersed with descriptions, feelings and realization of personal growth.[18]

Your Radar for Authentic Blue Communicators

Authentic Blues' communication style usually always involves **gestures**. They are so inspired and enthusiastic about their insights, their analogies and building a relationship that they are naturally animated, moving their hands frequently. Their hands are often extended and open as though they are embracing you, along with the world. Or, they may be clasped in a fashion as though they are literally trying to "hold together two halves of a message."[19]

Movement for these kids has its moments! If they are really focused on what they are telling you these children may actually bump into a table or the wall. They get so caught up in their imaginations and their stories that their parents will often tell us stories such as: "It's as if they don't even see the wall, or the stairs or the dog in front of them!"

Oftentimes these children tend towards being somewhat non-conformist, wanting to be unique, and will communicate this through their **appearance**. They may wear an unusual piece of jewelry, a scarf, shoes, something that makes a fashion statement — their own! These are the children that love finding a trunk in an attic filled with old clothes and vintage jewelry that they can re-configure to wear in a unique style. It is their way of playing with fashion.

Generally these children are well mannered, warm and personable in **demeanor**. They have an open and friendly attitude. Their warm, nurturing attitude makes them great communicators who, even as youngsters, listen empathetically, and often respond by touching others in a positive way. Their tone of voice is somewhat mellow and soothing, yet exciting at the same time since they can get very caught up in telling you about their dreams, their hopes, and their aspirations. They may disclose their personal, private thoughts, especially if they are extraverts. Ironically, because they are often lost in their own thoughts, others, such as their teachers, may describe them in terms of being detached from the real world and somewhat dreamy. As one parent told us, "The teacher sometimes has to say "earth to Jamie" to get a response!"

Our hope is that you will "live happily ever after" with your Authentic Blues the same as Ariel eventually does on land with her daughter! Their imaginative way of speaking about their hopes and dreams will always remind us of the little mermaid who dreamed one day of growing up and living in another land with her true love.

GPS for Resourceful Oranges' Communication Style

"The moment you doubt whether you can fly, you cease for ever to be able to do it."

"All you need is faith and trust, and a little bit of pixie dust!"
~Peter Pan

As a family we all fell in love with Peter Pan. Kate, especially, fell in love with him one year at Walt Disney World® Magic Kingdom® Theme Park; where she, literally, bumped into him... Really! They sat down and chatted for a short while. She found him to be quite charming! He captured her heart. Really, he has captured everyone's heart! We loved him in the book, in the Disney movie and on the Disney ride. Peter Pan is representative of Resourceful Oranges, so let's see what it is about their communication style that made us fall in love with Peter Pan...

Many of the great poets and public speakers are Resourceful Oranges. David Keirsey names a few: Byron, Dylan Thomas, Winston Churchill, Ronald Reagan.[20] Others that may be on the list? Mozart? Steven Spielberg? Emilia Earhart? Magic Johnson? Paul McCartney?

Words and Action Reflect Communication Style

"What is ..."

Like Organized Golds, Resourceful Oranges are natural observers who generally speak in concrete, practical terms, and talk about **"what is"** happening now. Your Resourceful Oranges will likely talk about their toys, their experiences, their practices, their fashions, their visits to friends, details, but not plans. Theirs is a "casual and uncomplicated communication style"[21], that often includes vivid descriptions of true life experiences. Their words seem to flow out of them easily and in an uncontrived way. For example, once our Resourceful Orange daughter attended school we always knew what was going on in the classroom, the extracurricular activities, what her friends were up to, etc. She made it her business to know who was doing what and what was happening, and then she reported it all at dinner! These children are naturals at networking!

Resourceful Oranges have an ear for sound. David Keirsey suggests that their paragraphs "are in effect songs".[22] They instinctively know what sounds good. That's what makes for good poets, orators, speech makers and song writers. Audiences love to listen to them. Just as we enjoy Peter Pan's quip, "all you need is faith and trust, and a little bit of pixie dust." Listen to your Resourceful Orange children's speeches, or read their essays, both of which may flow surprisingly well and sound good.

Resourceful Oranges' way of speaking is in keeping with their active traits. The symbol for this group is an exclamation point! They speak quickly, almost like they are talking in bullet points. They are usually in a hurry to get to the next adventure, to do the next thing, so they have to be quick when they are talking to you. They use contractions more than the other groups, allowing them to put two words into one — "would not" is usually "wouldn't" — and they may slur two words into one — "don't know" becomes "dunno."

Resourceful Oranges look for fun, adventure and action. Remember Peter Pan never wanted to grow up because he was having too much fun! They will turn what the other personality dimensions may see as simple, everyday occurrences into funny anecdotes. And they are usually anecdotes — not stories — because stories take too long to tell! For example, one Resourceful Orange mom told us about the first day of puppy training with their sweet, placid pup, "She was the mellowest dog by far. My children made up for the mellowness. While Joey (the dog) picked up 'sit' on the first try, my 10-year-old son did not!"

We have observed that Resourceful Oranges are usually aware of the latest trends in words. It's as though they have radar that "catches" these trendy words and they immediately "try them on for size" when they are speaking or writing. Once these new trends become mainstream they tend to stop using them, seeking the impact of new trendy words. Kate has a theory that often the trending words are created by Resourceful Oranges! As we write this book the word "selfie" has just been officially added to the dictionary. "Bestie" is another trendy word used often. Think back to when you first heard someone say one of these trendy words. Was that person a Resourceful Orange? Two words they use frequently are *"awesome"* and *"cool,"* and both are usually said with a lot of excitement!

"What works ..."

Resourceful Oranges usually get what they want by doing **"what works"** in an effective way. They think about what works and what fits for them, and then use it. If it is not currently useful or practical then they would say something like, "I don't need it." For them, "what works" takes precedence over "what's right," although they do tend to appear to be following what's right — in other words — the rules — while trying to somehow get around them! Since they tend to live in the moment your Resourceful Orange offspring may just "test the waters" and try something that may work, without putting a lot of thought into it or worrying about the consequences! These are the kids who might be angry with you at the moment, pack their bags, and start walking down the street, saying something like, "I'm running away!" with no thought as to where they are going or what they will eat for their next meal, or whether it is the right thing to do!

They think and speak in a style that is specific, definite and solid, while they use very practical ways to make their point. For example, your child may tell you, "I'm going on a field trip to ..." They don't tend to check with you or ask your permission, but rather inform you, since they clearly want to go on the field trip. After all, if they asked, you might say no! They figure it is worth a try to simply state what works for them. If that doesn't work they will come up with something else since this is, after all, the resourceful group!

Journal Sample: If your Resourceful Orange kid send you e-mails don't be surprised by their brevity. It is common for this dimension to get straight to the point, focusing on what is relevant. They are usually on the move, having to write a few additional quick messages or running to do something. If they keep a journal they will likely write about their own daily experience and sometimes include experiences of others, along with how they feel. Here is a short transcript from Kate's article on journal writing that reflects writing by a Resourceful Orange: Tina, who is popular and has a network of friends, is frustrated by her classmates who are not part of the chorus. She writes "A lot of people from my class are acting so bad and different and they won't fill Cheryl and I in on gossip. We feel so left out. I shouldn't really care because I'll be living a normal life one day (maybe)."[23]

Your Radar for Resourceful Orange Communicators

In general this personality dimension is very animated and will often make hand **gestures** while speaking. The common one is "a pawing motion ... the more aggressive gestures include the closed fist ... the index finger used to jab ... and the index finger used to peck"[24] at you.

If they seem to be quietly sitting, listening to you, they will often be "playing" with something. One Resourceful Orange parent confessed to us in our seminar that while he had been sitting quietly he had taken the eraser out of the top of the pencil and was playing with it the whole time! It seems that this very active group needs to be in **motion** most of the time, just like Peter Pan! Even while talking to you it appears as if they are going to move to something else, or to somewhere else. It is as though they just want to be free to move whenever and wherever they can. If these kids don't have an item to play with, or something exciting to do, they will fidget with whatever is available: they may pick at their nails, tap their fingers, or even chew on their own hair!

Just as they communicate with the trend-setting words, they want to have a trend-setting, even "flashy" **appearance**. They want to look good so are attentive to details. For example, their latest style jeans must fit perfectly. One grandmother told us she gave her 6-year-old Resourceful Orange granddaughter a t-shirt with a giraffe on it; a headband was painted on the giraffe with a real cloth flower attached to it. The six year-old was so impressed that she hugged the t-shirt and then kissed the flower. These kids love details in their clothes, even at six! This group is usually comfortable in their own skin, and insists on a comfortable way of dressing. Being active by nature, they don't want to be restricted! So they may choose runners over other shoes because they can move fast in runners, but the runners must be the latest trend!

With their quick movements and constant activity it is fascinating that this dimension tends to have a somewhat relaxed **demeanor**! They usually embrace life in a simple, easy-going way. Their fun-loving spirit is infectious and makes them enjoyable to be around. Their relaxed demeanor leaves them poised to act in the moment. Yet, they are usually great crises managers! Kate always says that these are the people who will get you out of a burning building with their fast thinking, fast moving, in-the-moment approach to living.

We hope you appreciate the children in this personality dimension just as much as we all enjoyed fun-loving Peter Pan. Their quick, animated way of speaking and moving will forever remind us of Peter Pan, the boy who never wanted to grow up!

GPS for Inquiring Greens' Communication Style

"She's safe, just like I promised. She's all set to marry Norrington, just like she promised. And you get to die for her, just like you promised. So we're all men of our word really ... except for, of course, Elizabeth, who is in fact, a woman."

(Standing on a cliff edge) "You know that feeling you get when you're standing in a high place?... sudden urge to jump? ... I don't have it."

~Jack Sparrow, Pirates of the Caribbean

Long before the release of Disney's first *Pirates of the Caribbean* movie (2003) featuring Jack Sparrow, our family enjoyed the Disney ride of the same name. We made sure to ride it every time we visited the Walt Disney World® Magic Kingdom® Theme Park. The movie was released, the ride was revamped (2006) and now included Jack Sparrow, one of the nine pirate lords in the Brethren Court, the Pirate Lords of the Seven Seas. When our grandson met the treacherous, scary looking pirate he was very young and somewhat mesmerized by Jack's outfit, including his sword, and his pirate "talk."

Jack Sparrow is our Disney representative for Inquiring Green; let's see how their communication style differs from the other three temperaments...

Albert Einstein is probably the most famous Inquiring Green. David Keirsey,[25] adds Victorian Prime Minister Benjamin Disraeli, anthropologist James Frazer, and the character Henry Higgins in Pygmalion. Other possibilities: Stephen Hawking? Thomas Edison? Madame Curie? Ayn Rand? Lewis Carroll? David Letterman? Walt Disney?

Words and Actions Reflect Communication Style

"What's possible ..."

Inquiring Green children naturally lean towards their imagination when thinking and, like Authentic Blues, their words are more abstract and they talk about **"what's possible."** They too may observe real things but often think of them as somewhat irrelevant to what is going on in their world of thoughts and insights. One Inquiring Green told me that he believed "it is somewhat absurd to discuss the weather when all you have to do is look outside! There are far more interesting topics that come to mind."

They too want to think of things beyond what is around them. Unlike the Authentic Blues who fantasize, these more curious Inquiring

Greens speculate about possible changes they can create to make things work better. No wonder their symbol is the question mark. They often use "if ... then" sentences much like inventors do. For example, one child inventor — Jeanie Low, aged 5, thought if she had a fold-up stool under the sink then she could unfold it to stand on it to reach the sink. Jeanie got a patent at eleven years old for *The Kiddie Stool.*[26]

Their reasoning may take precedence over facts and data, unlike Organized Golds who draw their conclusions based on the facts they have collected. For example, one Inquiring Green pre-teen concluded that it is time we eliminate gas for vehicles. When the grandparent pointed out that currently that might be difficult with so many cars on the road still using gasoline as fuel, the teen waved a hand as though to say that fact was irrelevant to his logical conclusion.

Inquiring Greens try to make others understand their complex thought process through their language. For many, like Jack Sparrow in the example above, their sentences may be so long and their ideas so complex that their listeners may lose track of their logic. Then they may draw a diagram to explain since they themselves have not lost track.

If that doesn't work they may, like Authentic Blues, resort to metaphors and analogies. Shakespeare's play, *As You Like It*, provides a great example: "All the world's a stage, And all the men and women merely players; They have their exits and their entrances..."[27] Yes, even their metaphors can be complicated! Inquiring Green children may like these metaphors: "your computer is a doorway to the Internet," "the science fair was a whale of a good time,"[28] "I felt like a dog with two tails," "he ran around like a headless chicken."[29]

They work hard at making you understand their concepts and ideas through their language. They choose words and phrases carefully as they think how to construct their argument logically. You will often hear words such as "likely, probably, usually, occasionally, and in some degree"[30] because they seem to know that there is always another way to see things. As your Inquiring Green offspring grow up they will often speak "tech-talk," which means that the conversations will become more and more technical. Generally they prefer "tech-talk" to small talk!

You may find your Inquiring Green child reading through dictionaries and Google word meanings because they enjoy learning about words and also adding words to their ever-growing vocabulary. They like long, complicated words. They learn exact definitions so they can then use them to make their listeners understand exactly what they are communicating. They will correct anyone, including you, who use an incorrect word! They don't mind being called "nitpickers," they just want to use the precise, exact word.

This colour group has their playful side when it comes to language, smartly teasing with their words, just as Jack Sparrow does in the second example above. They enjoy puns. Our young Inquiring Green grandchild regales us often with them! Examples include: "Q: Why wouldn't the skeleton climb the mountain? A: He didn't have the guts to do it!" or "Q: Why did the baby snake cry? A: She lost her rattle!;" or "Q: Who was Dorothy looking for in the desert? A: The Lizard of Oz!"[31] These children also love double meanings such as these examples: "he caught my eye," "bear with me," "toast the bride."[32]

In terms of writing, the Inquiring Greens make their points systematically using a great deal of logic. The older they get the more complex the sentence structures become, making it somewhat difficult for some of us to read. You can imagine how technical they could be in writing, with specifically-chosen words.

"What works ..."

Like Resourceful Oranges, this personality dimension usually attempts to get what they want by doing **"what works,"** while very aware of the social conventions and rules. However, Inquiring

Greens usually go about making it work a little differently. This group thinks about whether their ideas will wind up being efficient, with little interest in conventions or rules. They will brainstorm many ideas, eliminating some quickly because they cannot figure out an efficient way of using them. For example, one young Inquiring Green expressed the opinion that it might be useful and cost effective to heat the family home with solar energy. They then realized it would be too expensive to convert, and decided that it was a waste of resources for a house that was already built.

Inquiring Green children seem almost to be on a mission to make the world work better, more efficiently; often going against the grain of societal norms. When it comes to getting their work done in school this attitude can be problematic. For example, they may gather the facts from a variety of resources and then draw their own conclusions about what works for a science project. But then they don't see why their teacher makes them write a report on it! For them it is not an efficient use of their time when they have already learned what they need to learn and could be working on something else more interesting. They may also argue about routines with you for this same reason. For example, why go to bed at a prescribed hour if they are working on a project that seems far more important to them than getting a good night's sleep.

Journal Sample: This sample reflects writing as an Inquiring Green.[33] See if you can pick up on the "If ... then" way of thinking, along with "it's a waste of time" thinking. Harleen writes in her journal: "... we had a fidget contest where we couldn't move for one minute. A couple of people moved but not me; it was stupid and boring."

Kate read all the entries and made comments back, so this is Kate's response to Harleen: "I asked: I wonder why you would have a fidget contest. Any ideas?"

Harleen's response: "Because when we are not singing and Joseph or someone else is, we can't move because the focus is on Joseph.

If we move the audience looks at us and we get in trouble from the conductor." This is a great example of wanting the rationale to make sense and considering the consequences of her actions.

Your Radar for Inquiring Green Communicators

Inquiring Greens are not generally animated when speaking, making **few gestures**. They usually choose not to show emotions, staying cool, calm and collected while speaking. This gives the listener the notion that they are in control of their speech and their thoughts as they outline their latest ideas. They do get somewhat excited at times, usually about ideas, and will move their hands in a precise, controlled way that reflects their language pattern. "They bend their fingers and grasp the space in front of them... they use their fingers like a calculator, ticking off point after point ... (and they put their) thumb against their finger tips as if... bringing an idea... to the finest possible point."[34] They may also move inanimate objects around (e.g., salt and pepper shakers and glasses on a table), providing you with a visual of what it is they are trying to show you.

Like gesturing, their **movement** is generally not animated either. Theirs is a calm, cool, collected way of moving, demonstrating little emotion one way or another.

Inquiring Green children often get so caught up in their thoughts and ideas that they don't think as much about **appearance** (e.g., Einstein's famous hair). Some may not realize that their clothes look disheveled and may need reminders to look after their health and hygiene. One mother disclosed that she must insist that her son take showers and have haircuts, telling him, "This is not a debatable point!" We once visited Edison's home; apparently he installed a pool for his family that he never used because he didn't care to exercise, and was interested only in the body part above his neck! Other Inquiring Green children, on the other hand, may want to look the part of the intelligent person and so may dress to impress the world. For them, dressing the part is another competency they realize they need to develop. Your Inquiring Green child may want to appear successful and may eventually show great interest in expensive cars, designer clothes, and even fine dining!

That cool collected **demeanor** tends to come across in the tone of voice they use as well — almost like a neutral tone — not excited, not angry. As they grow older this tone may be misconstrued by some people as one of cold arrogance. The coolness in their tone may give way to one of irritable sarcasm if your Inquiring Green children are stressed.

As we give a hearty farewell to Jack Sparrow, we hope that you will continue to be amazed with your Inquiring Greens who, like Jack, use wit rather than weapons or force to communicate!

It is now time to switch gears. We are going to take a look at the "Innies" and the "Outies" (Introversion and Extraversion) as we continue our journey in the next chapter.

Chapter 7

GPS FOR INTROVERTS AND EXTRAVERTS ON YOUR JOURNEY

"My story begins in London, not so very long ago. And yet so much has happened since then, that it seems more like an eternity. ... As far as I could see, the old notion that a bachelor's life was so glamorous and carefree was all nonsense. It was downright dull."

~Pongo, the father, One Hundred and One Dalmatians

"Everything you see exists together in a delicate balance. As king, you need to understand that balance and respect all the creatures, from the crawling ant to the leaping antelope."

~Mufasa, Simba's father, The Lion King

You likely used your GPS to decipher the "colour" of the two "fathers" above from Disney movies. Pongo is a Resourceful Orange; and you will discover Mufasa's "colour" later in this chapter. Now did you notice anything else? One of the Disney "dads" exhibits introverted tendencies while the other exhibits extraverted tendencies. Which is which, you ask? Good question.

We are now going to expand your *GPS for Navigating Your Kids Personality* to include recognizing the **difference between Introversion and Extraversion**. We are pleased that *Personality Dimensions*® added the Introversion/Extraversion aspect of personality theory, since we believe the Introversion/Extraversion component is an important link to understanding human development. In her book, *Quiet*, Susan Cain confirms its importance by telling her readers that "introversion and extraversion are two of the most exhaustively researched subjects in personality psychology, arousing the curiosity of hundreds of scientists."[1]

Once you have gained a true understanding of the Introversion/Extraversion dynamic, it's time to call on your **radar detection**. This section will give you a fun, quick questionnaire to discover whether your offspring belong to the "Inny" (i.e., Introverted) or the "Outy" (i.e., Extraverted) group.[2]

To mix it up a bit in this part of our journey we will take you on **short road trips** of vignettes. For each of the four dimensions you will meet an "Inny" and an "Outy." Although it can be argued that preferences for Introversion and Extraversion are not always easy to spot, the examples here will be basic ones to give you a good idea of what you are looking for when it comes to your own children. To add to the fun, you will find a Disney character that exemplifies the personality dimension and the introverted or extraverted tendency, as described in the Disney blog.[3]

Are you ready then for your GPS excursion into introversion and extraversion? First we will explore the two terms, followed by cues to add to your radar detection to identify whether your offspring belong to the "Inny" or "Outy" group. And finally have some fun with short "road trips" to explore the introverted/extraverted preferences for each personality dimension.

Introverts and Extraverts: What's the Difference?

How can you tell whether you are living with an introvert or an extravert? Parents may answer something like this, the *Introvert is "quiet" and the Extravert is "talkative."* As parents ourselves, we had one of each and sometimes used these terms too.

If you think of your child as "quiet" or "shy" then you may be thinking in terms of youngsters who seem to be a little afraid of people, especially strangers, rarely say much to anyone, and pretty much stay quietly in the corner, perhaps even cowering a little.

On the other hand, if you think of your children as "talkative," then you may be thinking in terms of youngsters who rarely seem to stop long enough to think, preferring to blurt out whatever goes through their minds, constantly chattering to anyone and everyone who will listen, while rarely listening themselves.

Does that mean children will either want to be alone all the time or want to be with people all the time? Not really. All human beings need some time alone and some time with others. The real question is how much of each does your child need in order to thrive in his/her world? That will answer the question, Introvert or Extravert, more fully.

How then do we define Introverted children and Extraverted children in a way that will help them thrive?

You can turn back a century to discover that Carl Jung provided us with the answer in his book, *Psychological Types*, written in 1921. His elaborate outline of the concept revolved around energy. Yes, ENERGY! In *Nurture by Nature*, the authors provide a brief but effective way of thinking about introversion, extraversion and energy, based on Carl Jung's work. "Extraverts are generally energized more by being around other people, often the more the merrier.... Introverts are generally energized by getting away from other people and thinking their own thoughts."[4]

Therefore, we will refer to children more energized from within as "Innies," while those more energized from outside themselves as "Outies" — a fun way to think of your kids. Let's see how you might easily recognize the differences between your "Inny" and "Outy" children.

"Innies"

Children who are introverts — or "Innies" — can attend school all day and handle being in a classroom with others quite well. However, when they come home it is as if they turn the energy switch off. They often want time to focus their personal energy, mainly on the "inner world of ideas, people, thought, feelings and impression."[5]

They may just sit still and initially not say very much or talk at all. And they likely don't want to answer a lot of questions as soon as they come in the house. They may read or watch a favourite television show. They may play a solitary game or have a quiet conversation with you. "They choose solitude over social activities by preference, whereas shy people avoid social encounters out of fear."[6] This is how Innies revive, re-energize, re-fuel. It is not about being anti-social. It is not about being shy. It is about thriving — their way.

"Outies"

On the other hand, children who are extraverts — or "Outies" — attend school all day and then may want to continue the people stimulation in some manner. They may have had to be quiet in school all day too. They usually choose to focus their personal energy on the "outer world of events activity and things."[7] They may want to "talk your head off," as Kate's mom used to say, as soon as they get in the door, since they have been focused on school work much of the day. They might be ready to explode with conversation! Or, they might just be thinking "out loud" and seem to be rambling but often this helps them to figure out what they need to do next.

They may want to toss their backpack inside the door and "hang out" with friends or siblings, play a quick pick-up game of ball, etc. They re-fuel by being with people and doing things together.

Once again, understanding and encouraging your children to "step into their own selves" or be 100% themselves includes encouraging them to feel good about their natural inclination towards Introversion or Extraversion. There is no right or wrong tendency. Yet it has been argued that "our social conventions can be so rigid, they often don't allow for a child's natural comfort."[8] Your children are "hard-wired" to lean towards either the introverted or extraverted persuasion. Susan Cain makes a good argument for requiring both Introverts and Extraverts in society. She believes that they complement one other, providing examples of powerful Introvert/ Extravert pairings (e.g., Introverted Rosa Parks and Extraverted Martin Luther King Jr. who both had key roles as American Civil Rights Advocates), arguing that "Introversion plays yin to the yang of Extraversion."[9] Time to discover your kid's tendency.

Radar Detection for Your Kids: "Inny" or "Outy"?

Still not sure whether your child is like approximately thirty per cent of the North American population that calls themselves an Introvert or whether they fall into the majority-rules category of Extravert?[10] We decided to have a little fun, think of some examples for kids and paraphrase some of the introvert examples from *Splash*, written by one of our favourite Introverts, and colleague, Carole Cameron.

Do you find your child agreeing to the majority of these?

• They wonder how soon they can leave the party without anyone being upset

- They would prefer that you drive them to a birthday party rather than share a ride with a friend's parent
- They practice or think through what they want to say before saying it to someone important (e.g., a teacher, an employer)
- They have a short list of really good friends and tend not to "hang out" with new people
- They find talking with new kids in the community or at school tiring and hard work
- They use you as an escape strategy when other kids want them to stay later at school or at parties
- They wait for others to come say "hi" to them in group settings
- They like to think before they speak
- They don't mind lulls in conversations; it gives them time to think of what to say next
- They are very passionate about one or two subjects that aren't necessarily shared by their peers

If your child would answer YES to the majority of the above examples then they most likely have an Introverted preference, like Pongo, the father in 101 Dalmatians. They prefer to "focus on the meaning they make of the events swirling around them."[11] They are in good company with the following people who are often perceived as, or have disclosed that they are indeed, Introverts: Einstein, Newton, W.B. Yates, Dr. Seuss (Theodor Geisel), Charles Schulz, Meryl Streep, Johnny Depp, Carly Simon, Steven Spielberg, J. K. Rowling, Larry Page (co-founder, Google), and Pete Cashmore (founder of Mashable).[12]

If your child would have answered NO to the majority of the above examples they are most likely an Extravert, like Mufasa, Simba's father, in The Lion King. They want to "plunge into the events themselves."[13] They are in good company, with the following people who are often perceived to be Extraverts: Muhammad Ali, Margaret Thatcher, Bill Clinton, Nelson Mandela, Pope Francis and Walt Disney.

A caveat that we believe is helpful, before moving on is that Carl Jung believed that no human being is either 100% Introverted or 100% Extraverted. Indeed, Jung said, "Such a man would be in the lunatic asylum."[14] That being said, "Extraversion or Introversion is probably the most easily observed preference early on, yet it is often the least understood."[15] Let's see if we can help you by taking you on four short road trips to explore the differences.

Short Road Trips

Have fun with the four colourful "road trips" below; in each you'll be introduced to two children -- an "inny" and an "outy." These are basic examples so you can have some fun testing your GPS to decide on the colour and the introverted/extraverted tendencies described. You will also find the name of a Disney character for each scene as a suggested representative of each. You will find the answers at the end of each road trip. Enjoy!

The Birthday Party

Birthdays are exciting for kids. In the following two vignettes choose the colour dimension and whether the main character in each is an "Inny" or an "Outy."

Scenario 1: Jan, seven years old, in Grade 2, has one close friend, Lexie, in her class. Lexie invited Jan to her afternoon birthday party, mentioning that there would be lots of activities and 12 other kids attending, including many of whom she probably didn't know from Lexie's old neighbourhood. Jan wanted to attend because it was Lexie's party. However, she felt her energy drain just thinking about all of those other girls and boys whom she didn't know, and the length of the party! She spoke to her mother about her concern.

Jan's mom had a couple of *GPS* strategies to help. First of all, she had Lexie compile a list of attendees and reviewed the list with Jan, talking about how Jan might know some of the kids from other clubs and programs she had been in over the years. Together, they also decided that there was one other girl from the class, Meghan, whom Jan would be comfortable hanging out with at the party. Jan's mom emailed Meghan's mom, letting her know about their plan. On the day of the party, Jan was allowed to go a little earlier to help Lexie with the party set up and to be with her alone. She could then observe the other children arriving, rather than being one of the last ones to show up.

At the party, Jan hung out with Meghan, talking about the party and enjoying one another's company, even sharing the name of one another's imaginary friend. Jan had fun at the party because it turns out she did know many of the other kids, if only superficially, which made her feel comfortable participating in some of the events. She and Meghan worked on their respective craft together, chatting quietly about how to do it and what colours to use. They helped Lexie's younger sister create her craft too. They also enjoyed helping Lexie's mom in the kitchen for awhile, putting cupcakes on the plate in a decorative way while some of the kids played a game of soccer. She even disclosed her dream of being a writer of childen's fantasy books one day, since she loves myths, fairy tales and fantasy stories herself.

After the party, Jan quietly told her mother; "I am really tired but I had a great time with Meghan. I liked all the kids and am so happy that I went to Lexie's party!" Her mother wisely drove her home without "pumping" Jan for more information. Later Jan disclosed the meaning behind the picture she created at the party, how the chocolate cupcakes tasted like "a little bit of heaven," and that Lexie's mom is a great mom who wanted to hear about the stories Jan might write when she grows up.

Jan's colour? _____   Introvert or Extravert? _____

Hint: Disney character: Belle (Beauty and the Beast) or Pocahontas

Scenario 2: Something else was happening at Lexie's party. Jack, one of the boys who was invited, arrived late. Deep down, this upset him since he didn't want to let Lexie down. However, as soon as he took off his coat, he quickly surveyed the room, found the group of boys and joined them in watching a video. While watching the video, he was also scanning the room to see who else was at the party, what they were up to and who they were "hanging out with." At the end of the video, he was eager to work at the craft everyone was doing, and he chose to join some girls whom he knew he could chat with as he worked. As the activity progressed, he encouraged them to do their best and create something beautiful they could take home. When it was time for a quick game of soccer, Jack quickly volunteered to be a team captain and chose boys and girls whom he thought could use a confidence boost. He was energized by this role and enjoyed the opportunity to develop team unity and maximize the strengths of each player on the team. Finally, when it was time for cake and ice cream, Jack asked to be the ice cream scooper, so he would be able to connect with everyone and also help out.

At the end of the party, Jack was a little tired physically but energized by all the fun he had had. His dad picked him up and used a couple of *GPS* strategies to follow up. First of all, he asked about how Jack had done and what positive experiences came out of the party. Jack outlined how he helped some girls with their crafts and he loved the paint colours because they looked like a rainbow spread on the table. He enjoyed playing soccer with some old friends and new friends, and got a chance to be a team captain, which he had never been before. He said that Lexie's mom said he had helped out all afternoon and that made him feel particularly happy. His dad responded with praise and appreciation; Jack chatted the whole way home.

Jack's colour? _____   Introvert or Extravert? _____

Hint: Disney character: Aladdin (Aladdin) or Mufasa (The Lion King)

In these scenarios, we surmise that Jan is an Introverted Authentic Blue child whose need for only one or two close friendships is paramount and that she derives her energy from within. Jack, we feel, is also an Authentic Blue child, but he displays much more of the Extravert characteristic of deriving energy from those around him. Both children like to engage others in developing their human potential. Remember, though, that we are all a blend of the four dimensions and this also holds true for the Introvert/Extravert affinities. While our dominant tendency may to be introverted, we do, at times, have our extraverted moments, and vice versa.

Going to Camp

Summer vacation means a change in routines, time away from school life and often more family time. A favourite activity for many children is going away to camp for a week or two.

Scenario 1: Winston, age 13, has been eagerly awaiting his first day at Camp Forestgreen. This will be the fourth year in a row that Winston has attended this summer camp, so he knows it will be a great experience, just like his other three times. For weeks now he has been writing and revising his list of what to bring, and checking the items off the list when they are packed in his suitcase. Winston's dad had a couple of *GPS* strategies to help. He talked with Winston about campers' rules and responsibilities and has shown him a map of the area so Winston can really get "the lay of the land" now that he is one of the older campers. He also encouraged Winston to visit the camp website to make sure Winston is thoroughly acquainted with the programs he would like to participate in now that he is a senior.

Winston is looking forward to canoeing, golfing and horseback riding. He is also looking forward to participating in the ecoforest management team, having realized that he enjoyed group activities more this year in school because he rather likes the social interaction. Winston is already an accomplished swimmer, having progressed through various levels, and is thinking of challenging himself to join the swim team with some of his friends this year. He would like to try springboard diving this year too. Winston will be bringing his journal to record daily events and chart his progress in the activities he has chosen. As he approaches the first day of camp, he wonders if he will enjoy it as much as previous years and is really hoping that a couple of his close friends from previous years will be back again.

Winston's colour? _____ Introvert or Extravert? _____

Hint: Disney character: Cogsworth (Beauty and the Beast) or Cinderella

Scenario 2: Sasha, also age 13, is planning to attend the Forestgreen Girls Camp. She, too, is busy planning the experience, but her approach is a bit different. She wants to join the field hockey team, band, war canoe events, synchronized swimming and even beach volleyball. She has already emailed a bunch of her friends to see if a group of them can stay in the same cabin. She is charming so they all wanted to join her! She also has packed her cool and appropriate outfits for the camping experience. Since Sasha has attended this camp for a number of years as well, this year she would also like to begin Leader-In-Training lessons to help the junior campers.

Sasha's mom had a couple of *GPS* strategies to help. First of all, she is encouraging her daughter to re-examine the number of activities she has chosen, so that Sasha does not get over-extended. Her mom is also suggesting that Sasha take a favourite book or other individual activity when she has some "down time" from her busy schedule of events. Sasha believes that camp is a wonderful opportunity to contribute to the growth and development of pre-teens before they go to high school. She plans to write about this in her blog when she returns, and promises that she will text her family throughout the whole week!

Sasha's colour? _____ Introvert or Extravert? _____

Hint: Disney character: Maximus (Tangled) or Mary Poppins

In these scenarios, we surmise that Winston is an Introverted Organized Gold child whose need for planning and social responsibility is paramount and that he derives his energy from within himself. Sasha, we feel, is also an Organized Gold child, but she displays much more of the extraverted characteristic of getting energy from those around her. Both pre-teens like to show responsibility and appreciate the security of knowing what has worked well in the past will bode well for the future.

Science Centre Field Trip

Scenario 1: Elizabeth, aged 6, will be going to the Science Centre for the first time, with her Grade 1 class. For a few years now, Liz has demonstrated a love for anything mechanical and robotic. She is fascinated by puzzles, Lego, magnets, binoculars, bug catchers — anything that is interactive and "sciency." She has always been very inventive, inspired by stories her parents read to her, books on the human body, and how things work in general. She tells anyone who will listen that she will one day be an inventor and has already come up with a few ideas! Liz is gregarious and loves to share her science knowledge with everyone. In fact, she gets so excited and animated at times that she may interject her comments in others' conversations. To say the least, Liz is very keen on the upcoming science centre excursion with her whole classroom of friends.

Elizabeth's mother is aware of some *GPS* strategies that will be useful to ensure that the trip is a success. First of all, she has spoken with the teacher, requesting that Liz have a "buddy" who is a responsible listener and will be with Liz at the various exhibits. Secondly, she has reminded Liz that while she likes to be a leader that she must let the guide at the Centre talk and not interrupt constantly with her own "out loud" thoughts. Thirdly, mom also has told Liz that at dinner time, she can tell the family all about the highlights of the field trip, which mom knows will be all about the concepts she learns at the Science Centre.

Elizabeth's colour? _____ Introvert or Extravert? _____

Hint: Disney character: Jack Sparrow (Pirates of the Caribbean) or Shang (Mulan)

Scenario 2: Randy is in Liz' class and he too is keenly, yet quietly, excited about the trip to the Science Centre. His inquisitive nature and inner vision tend to make him thirst for more books and resources to quench his desire for knowledge. He learned to read at a very young age. His curiosity seems never ending and demands answers from his parents that they don't always have, even at this young age! He too "sees" the possibilities in what many consider ordinary objects. For example, he thinks his hat should have a built-in solar-powered heater, fearlessly telling adults that this would work! He spends much time deep in thought and may draw his ideas rather than verbalize with others, and while he generally doesn't appear to be very emotional towards his younger sibling, when he cries Randy goes to him and tries to help him.

Randy's father is aware of *GPS* strategies that may help ensure a successful trip for his son. Dad has given Randy a small sketch book and pencil to carry with him to draw some of the things that he sees that are of particular interest, which he may share with his dad after the field trip is over. His dad knows that Randy will likely absorb a lot of information, particularly anything on a global level that will lead him to thinking up yet more inventive ideas that he may share with his dad or his close friend. In addition, dad has also purchased a few age-appropriate books about global warming to encourage his son's strength and interests in this area, which his dad knows will be demonstrated at the Centre.

Randy's colour? _____ Introvert or Extravert? _____

Hint: Disney character: Elsa (Frozen) or Owl (Winnie the Pooh)

In these scenarios, we surmise that Liz is an Extraverted Inquiring Green child whose core need for knowledge and competence is in evidence and that she derives her energy from interacting with those around her and from demonstrating and verbalizing that knowledge. Randy, we feel, is also an Inquiring Green child, and he displays much more of the Introverted characteristic of getting energy from his inner self, preferring to draw some of his thoughts. In both of these children, we see the Green analytical and objective traits.

Beach Resort Vacation

Scenario 1: Bill (age 11) has just arrived with his family at a beach resort for a week's holiday. He has never been to a resort before so he is both excited and curious. The flight was over three hours long, and he had a difficult time staying seated and occupied — even his video games didn't sustain his interest for long — and he had to be relatively quiet on the plane, which was challenging for him. Now that he was at the resort he wanted to release some of his energy and do something – anything!!

Bill's dad knew a good *GPS* strategy would be to let him start exploring what the resort had to offer. Bill's mom offered to register while he and his dad set off. Bill quickly found the rock climbing area, the miniature golf, the swimming pool and the outdoor trampoline, which he immediately started jumping on, after quickly throwing off his shoes. He met a couple of other kids on the trampoline and was soon chatting and laughing as he bounced along with them. Before long, they had agreed to try to meet later for some time together on the rock climbing apparatus as well as a miniature golf competition, and he had already taken pictures of his new-found friends to add to his memory collection of photos which he had started snapping (of his family) as soon as they hit the airport. Bill's dad encouraged this interaction and made sure to input the names and room numbers of Bill's new-found friends into his cell while Bill chatted a little longer. As they were walking back to the resort lobby, Bill remembered his shoes and asked if he could run back to get them by himself, but his dad went too. Then Bill saw the arcade and started pulling his dad into it, saying, "just one game Dad!" He wanted to stay longer but his dad knew he had already spent enough of his allowed funds both at the airport (where he found presents for his extended family and friends back home) and at the arcade, telling him that he didn't need to spend it all on his first day of vacation!

Bill's colour? _____ Introvert or Extravert? _____

Hint: Disney character: Flynn Rider (Tangled) or Peter Pan

Scenario 2: Bill's cousin, Meredith, joined the family for the vacation. Meredith found the flight long and she too was a little restless, although much quieter about it than her cousin! When she arrived at the resort with the family, she soon found herself with her Aunt Sarah, doing the check-in duties, which she didn't mind because she liked spending quality time with her favourite aunt. But she also wanted to know what adventure might be in store for them at the resort.

Quickly sensing the pull Meredith had between running off on an adventure immediately or having some quiet time with Aunt Sarah, her aunt pointed out the adjacent rack of brochures, suggesting that she find some that would be of interest to her, while Aunt Sarah completed the registration (a good *GPS* strategy). Then the two of them went on their own short exploration of the resort. Meredith was keen on the swimming pools, the rock climbing apparatus, sailing and snorkelling, and the arts and crafts area. She could do these activities in a small group or with just the instructor. As she and her aunt wandered through the resort, she impulsively walked towards the "50's Malt Shoppe," pleading with Aunt Sarah "just this once" let her have a milkshake in the middle of the day, right before dinner, even if it meant using some of her money that was supposed to be saved for the next day! Her favourite aunt consented.

Meredith's colour? _____ Introvert or Extravert? _____

Hint: Disney character: Pumbaa (The Lion King) or Flik (A Bug's Life)

In these scenarios, we surmise that Bill is an Extraverted Resourceful Orange child whose core need for freedom and spontaneity is in evidence and that he derives his energy from interacting with those around him. Meredith, we feel, is also a Resourceful Orange child, but she displays much more of the Introverted characteristic of quietly getting re-energized after a long trip to the resort. In both of these children, we see the Orange need for action and quick decision-making, and impulsiveness toward spending!

Hopefully you will now recognize the differences in the Introverted/ Extraverted preferences within each dimension. It is our sincere desire that, no matter the tendency of your offspring, you encourage them to grow into themselves so they can thrive. Both Introverts and Extraverts can get stressed. Your extraverted children stress when isolated too long or having to sit for extended periods of time or from not getting clear directives. Your introverted children can be stressed with too much noise, too many people, public speaking and constant supervision. We leave this discussion with these positive words of wisdom, "humanity would be unrecognizable, and vastly diminished, without both personality styles."[16]

What's next? We end our journey where we started — back home. How do you now take everything you have learned about personality dimensions and create a comfortable atmosphere that embraces your children's needs and values?

Chapter 8

GPS FOR CREATING POSITIVE HOME LEARNING ENVIRONMENTS

As two educators, we feel that learning is an important facet of home life, since for much of the time you spend raising your children they are students. A home environment that takes their personality dimensions into consideration can decrease some of the angst of getting homework done, for both parent and child! As a teacher and administrator, Wayne maintains, "The school only has your kids for six hours a day, and not every day. The rest is up to you to encourage them in their roles as life-long learners." In this chapter we will describe how you can create a positive home environment that embraces your kid's learning style.[1]

Each dimension tends to have a **"go-to" question** they ask. They also each have a specific question about what it is they are learning.[2] We will explore how the two questions are related so you can address them before your kids even ask! We will also provide an example of what you can do to help them.

The four dimensions each have a specific **route to learning**. Parents find this helpful to know since, if it differs from their own approach to learning, they can address their children's needs better. As one parent told me, "I nag less because I get that my children don't approach learning the way I do."

You may wonder if there is a **"go-to" way to fuel learning** that supports and encourages children in each group. There is, and we will provide some ideas about how you can help make the job of getting homework done a little less problematic.

Getting there on time differs for each of the four groups. Knowing this allows you to guide them in learning time management tricks that work for them — to get their homework done on time. Time management is not about managing the 24 hours in a day so much as it is about managing yourself and your style.

Finally, to quote a line from the movie *Field of Dreams*, "If you build it, they will come!" Creating an **environment** or a **"reserved" learning space** that is conducive to your kid's homework habits can help alleviate some of the "homework wars."

We have switched this chapter a little, splitting it into topics, rather than into dimension groups. If you have more than one child you can explore a topic to quickly see the innate differences amongst your children. It is our hope that this chapter will be a culmination of all that you have gleaned about your offspring and will spur you into rearranging some of the ways you are currently doing things at home to accommodate the specific natures of your children.

The "Go-to" Questions

Organized Gold Learners: How?

Organized Golds tend to ask **"How?"** because they like to plan their lives. We suggest that the "How?" question goes deep in their core because they are happiest when they know how they can contribute to their families, to their classmates, and, ultimately, to society, to feel they belong in these respective groups.

Organized Golds feel great when they have certain duties and responsibilities assigned no matter what role they have accepted. In the student role, when they might not fully understand the reason to learn something, aside from out of respect for their teachers, they ask the question, **"How am I going to use this information?"** In other words, is there a purpose for me to learn this material? How will it ultimately help me to contribute to society? For these concrete learners there has to be a practical application.

Help them find practical applications by focusing on what they may need in the future or what their current choice of career might be and how they would utilize the information. For example, Kate's math teacher introduced two decimal points. Blank stares resulted. When he placed the dollar sign in front of the question the Organized Gold learners got it immediately! The reason to learn decimal points is to gain an understanding of currency, which is totally practical!

Authentic Blue Learners: Who?

The Authentic Blues tend to ask **"Who?"** because they are all about people and their purpose. We believe that the "Who?" question goes very deep in their core need because these children are happiest when they are surrounded by people who create harmonious relationships with them at home, at school and in society.

They feel great when they see that they are improving every day or that they can help others improve. They want to know, "How will learning this material make me better or make the world better around me?" In other words, **who will benefit?** They naturally look for authentic relationships. They thrive in interpersonal learning settings, especially when they see how their learning will benefit those who are around them.

Help them understand how learning something at school may have an application for them — or others — now or in the future. For example, one Authentic Blue student did not like science until a cancer researcher spoke to the class about his role in saving lives. Mom reminded this child that her mother (the child's grandmother) was a cancer survivor as a result of similar research, helping create a connection for her children, who now understood the relevance of science to humankind.

Resourceful Orange Learners: When?

Remember what makes Resourceful Oranges happy? Freedom! They often ask **"When?"** because they want to know when they can be free to act upon the latest idea. It goes deep into the core of the Resourceful Oranges who want freedom to be and do what they want to do. When? Immediately!

For these learners life is great when they can freely enjoy a variety of activities; they "shine in action!"[3] Learning new things in new ways can work for these active learners once they can answer this question: **"What can I do with this new material?"** They want to know when it will be useful to them, and when they will do something interesting with the new material. In other words, how is it practical and relevant.

These learners are easily bored with routine, so creating ways to make learning more fun works wonders. One parent told us that her child was learning about eating healthy fruits so she took her kids to a pick-your-own strawberry farm where they could pick and eat all they wanted. Imagine the freedom your naturally spontaneous and active Resourceful Orange learners would feel if they could eat handfuls of strawberries out in the field.

Inquiring Green Learners: Why?

Generally the Inquiring Greens most asked question is, **"Why?"** They are delighted with finding answers. The question "Why?" speaks to the very core of this naturally curious group.

For these learners a successful day means that they had an opportunity to display their competency. Their "go-to" question is: "How will this new material increase my competency?" In other words, **"Why learn it?"** These abstract thinkers thrive when they can learn independently and research their own interests, finding answers to their never-ending question, why? They embrace change, and enjoy new material, especially in the science and technology fields.

If these learners don't have an interest in the subject matter then they don't want to learn it. Parents have asked, "How do we get them to even start their homework in these subjects?" Provide them with "the big picture". One father told us of his child's desire to only check out the report card mark given in Science and Technology, thinking that is all that matters. This parent, however, pointed out that other subjects, even English, mattered, for example, because, "If you cannot read and communicate well it will be difficult to understand some of the more advanced scientific findings."

The Route to Learning

To understand more fully how each personality dimension approaches learning new material, Wayne asked a group of facilitators to tell us how they would put together a newly-purchased chair that comes in parts. In other words, the box is sitting in the middle of the floor unopened; what are you going to do with it? What do you need? What do you look for when you open the box? This is a practical experiment that demonstrates how each learning group goes about getting homework done.

With each component listed in their approach to learning we will tie in the "chair experiment" so you can see firsthand how each temperament group uses that element to get the job done.

Organized Golds' Route to Learning

Instructions are crucial to these learners. The Organized Gold facilitators in the chair experiment said that once they opened the box, they would pull out everything to find the "how-to's" (i.e., instructions). They would follow them explicitly, step by step, to "get the job done" efficiently. Your Organized Gold children want to know exactly how to do their assignments, which means the tasks must be clearly laid out for them to follow before they begin their homework.

The Organized Golds would also look for a picture, or better yet, go to the store and see the chair, before attempting to put it together. This is akin to the Organized Gold child needing a **solid foundation** from which to work. For example, in English literature, they will most likely have read the entire story before beginning to write an essay about it.

Next the facilitators said that they would place the parts in a row and count them to confirm that they had the correct number of parts prior to proceeding, according to the instruction sheet, that presumably would have provided this information. Similarly, the Organized Gold learners want to have all of their **resources provided**. Whether it is just pen and paper, or textbooks, or websites; they want to know that all of this is available prior to starting their assignments.

Organized Golds like to be efficient and so want to **do tasks correctly** the first time. That is exactly why the Organized Gold facilitators said that they would take time at the beginning of a project to read the instructions, make sure they know that they have the knowledge behind it and the resources with which to work before starting the project. Your Organized Gold learners also need to know that they have been provided with a solid foundation, effective instructions, and the materials so that they can get their homework done right the first time.

Finally, the Organized Gold facilitators wanted to receive a thank you for their specific answers about putting the chair together. As a parent, it is helpful to know that when the Organized Gold learners complete their tasks they want to be given **concrete recognition** for having done the work. You can give them check-marks, stars, beads, an allowance, whatever you decide on, in order to clearly demonstrate that they did the work. When viewing their projects they want to hear something like, "I like the way you set up that page." This feedback will propel them into completing the task today and in the future.

Authentic Blues' Route to Learning

Collaboration with others is crucial to Authentic Blue learners. In the chair experiment, the facilitators indicated that they would collaborate with someone. Your Authentic Blue offspring like working with others when learning. At home they want the support of family members; at school they want the support of peers, as well as the encouragement of the teacher. These learners may feel the teacher does not like them if their efforts are not affirmed, and sometimes for that reason will not want to do their homework.

Authentic Blues' learning style includes learning that is in some way **relevant to their lives**. The facilitators wanted to know who would be using the chair, for example. Some said that they would love to hear it is being donated to a women's shelter. Similarly, you get faster "buy in" from your Authentic Blue learners if you can show them the relevance or meaning behind the learning. For example, a Grade 5 student had no problem learning about fractions after they realized that this knowledge can then be applied to cooking/baking favourite family recipes.

Stories, metaphors, and analogies make learning come alive for the Authentic Blues, and often these children will identify with story characters. In the case of the chair, the facilitators would have enjoyed knowing the reason that this particular chair was chosen. The mother of one Authentic Blue learner told us, "stories seem to help them connect the dots" with what they are currently learning.

For example, you may find movies or books that depict historical eras, which they will particularly enjoy, that pertain to the history lessons at school. A former teacher, Jennifer Maruno, wrote *When the Cherry Blossoms Fell*, a novel for pre-teens which eloquently captures the struggles of a Japanese Canadian family after WWII.

Authentic Blues also learn well with **hands-on activities**. The facilitators said they wanted to get on with the actual building of the chair; in particular they wanted to work together. You can enhance your kid's learning by letting them apply some of their knowledge in the home. For example, when they are learning about fractions let them help cook a family favourite dinner with you or bake cookies with their friends after school. Or show them how decimals apply to shopping; try the math teacher's trick of placing a dollar sign in front of the decimals and see how quickly they understand that math lesson.

Finally, Authentic Blues enjoy **personalized feedback**. If the facilitators had put the chair together they would have wanted to know how much they personally helped to get the project done. At home you can demonstrate how pleased you are with the effort your kids put into working on their assignments, while letting them know that they are valued for themselves. It is all about them as people when it comes to feeling good about having completed work.

Resourceful Oranges' Route to Learning

Resourceful Oranges love to have **fun and adventure**. They are naturally playful. The facilitators thought it would be fun to turn it into a "let's put a chair together" party and order in pizza. Let your Resourceful Learners have a little fun in the midst of doing their homework; tell a joke or an anecdote and then get back to the homework to help make the work go better. It always helps to enjoy a fun snack break as well!

Visual resources work well for Resourceful Orange learners. When Kate mentioned the chair experiment to a group of parents, the Resourceful Oranges said they might take a look at the written instructions but would definitely go to YouTube to see if they could find someone showing them how to build the chair (particularly if it was a common big box chair model). It is helpful to know that your concrete Resourceful Orange learners will look at many resources that provide them with the freedom to pick and choose what they want to access. They prefer visual or multisensory resources over theoretical concepts. For example, one of the parents told us, "It always helped me if I could watch the movie after reading the book it was developed from to remember the story for exams."

Resourceful Oranges learn by **being active** and doing. In the chair experiment the parents assured us that they would enjoy actually building the chair. If your child can play a game to learn something new then they are all for it. Creating a game or a contest for them makes learning active. One grandfather told us how he helped his grandchildren understand comparisons. Together they created a chart with criteria for the best milkshake in town. They visited five shops and shared one milkshake at each shop. By the end of the day they had a winner. There was a lot of learning in the middle of this active (and very tasty) adventure for his grandchildren.

These learners like to have **clear directions** and clear expectations from others. The Resourceful Orange parents said that often the building instructions from big box stores may not be clear, which was another reason for checking its assembly on YouTube. These learners want to do the task quickly so usually like to just jump in and start. If they don't have any idea of how it is to be done, or your expectations, it helps if they know what they are supposed to do. Building a volcano for a science project, for example, would be fun but they would likely prefer to watch it being built on a video first.

Like all learners, Resourceful Oranges want **feedback**. They usually prefer it to be immediate, direct and open — with encouragement and support. Many parents tell us that saying "Awesome" when their Resourceful Oranges show them their work is all their kid needs.

Inquiring Greens' Route to Learning

The Inquiring Greens generally enjoy learning and want **intellectual challenges**. Just be careful to provide them with challenges that are within their level of competency, since they tend to doubt themselves already. Many Inquiring Green learners will choose to play challenging games on their various devices and enjoy moving up through the levels as they meet the challenge of each one. Sometimes they push themselves too much and end up frustrated because they don't feel "smart enough" to meet the challenge. In the box example, one Inquiring Green grandparent shared that he has watched his own Inquiring Green child look at a project like the chair (or in the child's case, a new Lego set), then "assess if the assembly procedure is obvious or not. If yes, then (his child) would proceed with assembly." In other words, his child would enjoy the intellectual challenge of putting it together without the instructions.

These learners are naturally curious and want to learn by having the **freedom to ask questions.** They have a thirst for knowing how things work (e.g., the human body, the computer, the engine). They also ask why things work the way they do. So they may ask things like, "Why can't dogs talk?", "Why can't cars fly?", "Why do we have to go to school to learn?" They will seek logical explanations to acquire a good understanding. Try to answer their questions honestly and directly, or steer them to sources where they can find answers. One parent told us that their child likes nothing better than to receive a book that goes into great detail about the human body, although when asked, her child did not necessarily want to be a health professional, but "just wanted to know." In the chair example, the Inquiring Greens mentioned that they would not hesitate to "scan the instructions" if it was not obvious how to assemble the chair. In other words, they felt free to ask, "how is it supposed to work?"

Inquiring Greens may choose to **extend the learning** that has been set out for them by their teachers because they want to know much more than is required. Initially you may need to help them find these extra resources to encourage them in this. Eventually you will find them researching for more and more information just because they want to acquire more in-depth knowledge. This is where you as parents need to do a balancing act between encouraging them and being patient with their natural inclination to acquire more knowledge than required, while at the same time ensuring that they do complete the assigned work! As one parent told us when her child receives fascinating books for presents he will sit right down to read them, forgetting that there is homework waiting to be completed. The good news is that once they are satisfied that their own questions have been answered, they move on to the next subject!

Inquiring Greens will work hard if it is a subject in which they are **interested**. In fact they may spend an unlimited amount of time and effort on that particular subject. For example, in the case of the chair, if the Inquiring Greens had been given the assignment to choose the chair and then assemble it they would have been truly interested in the project. They would have taken the time to research and choose a specific chair, after knowing its specific purpose. One parent did ask something like, "Why did you choose that particular chair?" He wanted to know more specifics and took a great interest in the project. Your Inquiring Green child may, in fact, not believe that some subjects are relevant to them so will need some direction in getting work done them. One Inquiring Green student only looked at the science and technology mark (an A) and had no regard for the other subjects (not one A in any of them). The parents in this case were quick to point out that other subjects have their place in his schooling and cannot be dismissed!

Inquiring Green learners often choose to learn **independently**. They want to approach the work the way they want to and not be tethered by being part of a group collaboration. In the case of assembling the chair, the Inquiring Green adults made it clear that they would simply open the box and start the process of assembly on their own and not even think about collaborating with anyone else. Working alone allows your child to explore, research, and figure things out for themselves. They want to find the resources, analyze them, think about the concepts behind them and then decide how to use their skills to complete the work. As one parent told us, the problem is their child enjoys the independent work so much that this child often creates his own projects just for fun, even when there is other work to be done!

When it comes to **feedback** remember that Inquiring Greens seek knowledge constantly and tend to be very analytical by nature. These learners want feedback to know specifically what is well done and what needs a little work. They want a critique of their work, and preferably delivered in a succinct way. In the case of the chair, one of the parents said that he would take the time himself to analyze its stability, ensuring there was no "wobble," and also ensure that he had each screw tightly in place, so it would not fall apart when someone sat on it. Your Inquiring Green kids are not looking for a personal, subjective style that is often more appealing to other personality dimensions. They just want a factual analysis so they can learn from the information.

Fuelling The Learning Journey

Fuelling Organized Golds' Learning

By nature these children are organized and neat; they like to plan ahead and be prepared for everything within their power. Helping your Organized Gold learner **create a concrete plan** of action will help maintain order for them. Organized Golds prefer structure; they want to create and follow a schedule, so they know that at a specific time of the day they will do their homework. They check off all tasks in their agendas as they complete them, ready for the following day.

Organized Gold learners usually follow rules easily, and look for the rules in the assignments. Help them create an **outline of reasonable expectations** to plan their time and effort accordingly.

For example, if they need to deliver a speech, they want to know the following: timelines for choosing the topic, writing the speech and delivering the speech; required length of the speech; and specific criteria for which they will be judged. They want to know how the winner will be chosen and what kind of recognition will be given to the winner and the runners-up. If there are regional competitions, they want to know the timelines for these as well. Once they have the expectations in mind they will begin writing the speech.

Help them develop their skills of organizing and **summarizing** more complicated information so they can fully grasp the information and not become overwhelmed with too many details. They generally enjoy charts and lists to organize information in a factual way that makes sense to them. A parent shared, "My child actually makes a list of her lists." The other parents groaned! Creating charts/lists helps them learn concepts and theories more easily. For example, in learning personality dimensions theory they could create a list of the differences and the similarities between their own nature and that of their best friend.

These children tend to learn well by **practicing** over and over again, so learn well by rote. They are like little beavers that will do the same thing over and over, so let them practice doing! For example, the scientific periodic table of elements has been put to music; what better way for an Organized Gold to learn that table (yes, it is on YouTube). It certainly makes the learning a little easier! The little ones learn their ABCs far faster if they sing the ABC song. It is a way for them to get the basic foundation before learning advanced concepts.

Organized Gold learners plan for tests and exams that are expected. But you may need to help them **prepare for unexpected quizzes**. Their ability to memorize details helps them retain information for those pop quizzes. For example, once they have the concept of a new math topic, have them do one or two sample questions without any help. This serves to build trust in their own memorization skills. Or, in the case of the speech they prepared, once they memorize it, have them give it to family members to build their overall confidence. Often they do not realize that they know something until put on the spot with a pop quiz or asked to give the speech to the family.

Fuelling Authentic Blues' Learning

Authentic Blues are naturally imaginative communicators with talents for speaking, writing, and creative thinking. All of these natural skills and abilities can help to provide them with a **positive perception** of homework. One concept that can help persuade them to do their homework is that they are helping their teachers by doing the homework, which works only if they like the teacher and feel the teacher is supportive of them. Another idea is that since they like to help people, let them help their peers if they express a desire to do so. The upside of this is that they will want to learn the material well enough that they can then help a friend better understand it. One parent told us of their Authentic Blue child who would ask him all kinds of questions about the car's engine because his child was trying to help someone better understand a concept in science.

These children often learn well through **interacting** with others. Let them have friends over to work together on projects or homework sometimes. By sharing together they will perceive learning and homework in a more positive way. Or do your work in the same room at the same time as they do their homework. Or have their siblings do their homework in the same room. These learners do not generally want to work in isolation. One Authentic Blue parent confessed that as an adult she had an office set up in her home but she preferred working at the kitchen table with others around her.

Authentic Blue learners may need your **help in staying on task** since they can sometimes get caught up in the stories or the background material. They may need help in reading the assignment to gain a clear understanding of how to answer the questions correctly. One teacher told us that these learners love the character development in books but may struggle with questions specific to the plot of a story.

Sometimes managing the amount of material to learn with all of the details can be overwhelming for these learners. However, they usually grasp concepts, theories and the "big picture" easily. They can learn to use this ability to create summaries, overviews or cognitive maps to organize and to **integrate information**. They can then visualize the information better.

Authentic Blues don't usually enjoy competition although they often are graded in a competitive fashion. You may want to monitor these learner types by helping them **focus on their own progress**. For example, suggesting that they should study to get a better mark than someone else in their class may not be the best way to get "buy in" to do the homework. Instead, you may want to try suggesting that now that they have specific organizational and studying skills, they could perform better on the next quiz than they did on their last quiz. This could help persuade Authentic Blue learners to manage their own progress and improve their performance.

Fuelling Resourceful Oranges' Learning

Inject new activities when it comes to learning. Resourceful Orange learners don't want to sit for long periods of time, so break it up by changing it up with different activities that will help energize them so they can finish the work. For example, they may have to do scales for piano practice or they may be learning a difficult piece of music. Let them have a change by playing a piece of music they particularly enjoy playing, or playing the scales to different rhythms, or taking a break altogether.

These learners want practical **concrete ways to apply theory** and "big picture" concepts. Help them develop skills to put theory into practice so they can understand the concepts better. Otherwise, they can get bored and not want to do the work. For example, Kate tutored a Resourceful Orange peer in calculus. He could not understand that "a" and "b" in an equation were different until she showed him an apple and a banana. The lights went on and he could do the homework.

Encourage your Resourceful Orange learners to **demonstrate their learning** through actions. They generally enjoy sharing experiences with you if you just let them. It might be something they learned in science that they want to demonstrate. Or you might want to further their knowledge by looking on-line for science experiments you can do at home together. If they play an instrument in band, let them play the piece they are rehearsing for you or for a favourite relative or family friend who is visiting. You might want to videotape them so they can watch themselves.

Winning a **competition** is just plain fun for these learners. The drudgery of getting an assignment finished could be turned into a competition between yourself and your child. Maybe you have a project you could be working on. By setting up a competition with a prize you could both get your work done! If the prize is something that they would really like, chances are they will work harder. In some cases, the prize might simply be staying up later to watch a favourite video, or in the case of teens, being allowed to stay out a little past curfew.

If they have a large project to do, have them work with you to break it down into much more doable sections. Resourceful Orange learners work well when you **chunk** their work. If for example, they need to draw and label a project for health it may seem like a lot of work to your child. You might suggest that they draw the picture one evening and label it the following evening. The older they get the more homework they will have to do so learning how to chunk the work and make it do-able each evening is an invaluable lesson for these kids who like leaving things until the last minute. It helps them use their tendency to rise to the challenge at the last minute if you give them deadlines for chunks.

Fuelling Inquiring Greens' Learning

Some parents have found that when these learners are bored or don't want to look at subjects they consider uninteresting, they can encourage their kids to **explore new things related** to the subject.

For example they may not like taking English but they may find it fascinating to learn how language has evolved and changed over the centuries. They may then gain an appreciation for the language. Inquiring Greens have a dry wit, so creating puns, for example, demonstrates a way of "playing" with the language.

They may need your help to demonstrate their knowledge in a **simplified format** using charts, flow charts and graphs to make it easier for others to understand. Sometimes they have too much interrelated information and have difficulty demonstrating what they know in a simple, direct manner. Help them ensure that they answer the question being asked. In a seminar Kate ran, a group of Inquiring Greens created an answer for her on a laptop using a green background with a logo they designed on the spot. It looked very impressive, however, they missed the target completely; they did not answer the question!

These learners enjoy conceptual analysis, so encourage them to choose projects that allow them to research theory. They like to think about **"connecting the dots"** so as they learn something new, they may want to think about how it relates to topics studied previously. Or they may want to write an essay that integrates information they learned in one subject with information gleaned from another. For example, they may be learning about healthy foods in one class and physical exercise in gym. They might enjoy researching how the two relate to the overall health of the human being.

Inquiring Green learners are naturally analytical. Using this inborn talent can enhance their learning. They may **analyze** the pros and cons of an issue; or they may challenge the information they read. They might analyze how they completed successful projects before, so they can replicate their actions. Encourage them to use these abilities to get the work done and to prove to themselves that they can finish projects by the due date.

These learners usually focus on the future and can be quite visionary. They often will tell you what their career will be at quite an early age, although they may tell you many different vocations over time! When Inquiring Greens have difficulty learning something new, it may seem to them that this material is isolated information of little value. Try to help them see how this material relates to interests or vocations in the future. When one Inquiring Green realized that running increases one's overall health and helps make stronger muscles, this youngster was delighted to join the running team at school.

Getting There On Time

Getting There on Time for Organized Gold Learners

Part of managing time for Organized Gold learners is setting goals for themselves. With a little help from you, they will like to do this from a very young age. For example, having them set **short time goals** such as 10 minutes to get their homework done in first grade will help them develop their natural planning and organizing skills effectively.

Over time they can then learn to set **long-term goals** that will provide a lot more time to achieve what they set out to do. These students are natural planners who want to figure out how they are getting from point A to point B. They may, for example, want to join a running club that meets every Thursday after school and culminates in a 3-kilometer run at the end of the semester. This gives them a concrete goal to look forward to and is a healthy way of learning to look after their bodies. By high school age, they may want to run in marathons, which will require good skills to manage their time to train, prepare for and run in marathons.

Organized Gold learners want **concrete timelines**; depending on their age, they may need you to help them with this. For example, if they need to travel with you to take a sibling to a rehearsal or practice, this needs to be built into their schedule; likewise, as teens, they may need to build time into their schedule to drive their sibling to practice. They will then know whether they can finish one subject at home prior to going out and complete another once they return home. While timelines may vary according to the day, Organized Golds will want to follow the same timeline each week for any given day.

Many Organized Gold parents tell us that they practically sleep with their **time device**, whatever form that may take. Furthermore, they cannot remember a time, even as youngsters that they did not want to know the time! So Organized Gold learners would really appreciate having a digital clock or watch to ensure that they keep on track. You may also want to use a timer for them, which many parents have told us are useful for these kids who always want to know, "how much longer?"

Getting There on Time for Authentic Blue Learners

These futuristic learners see the big picture and may have idealistic goals. Part of managing time for these learners is setting **realistic goals** as opposed to the idealistic, often overly positive goals they may set for themselves. For example, they may want to write a novel when they grow up, but meanwhile have not started the essay that needs to be written now for English class.

Your Authentic Blue child can get their homework done if they have manageable amounts so they don't feel overwhelmed. You may need to help them initially choose the subjects they must work on in a specific time limit. By **chunking** their work into manageable amounts of time they will realize that it is doable. For example, if they have math homework they might try chunking it, page by page, so they work on one page, take a break and go back to it. The break may be reading part of the story for English that they are enjoying, if math is not one of their best subjects.

Expect some daydreaming on the part of Authentic Blues. These sensitive learners may become distracted with ideas and stories as they connect the dots between the learning and its relevance. Be sure to monitor them and **keep them on track** so they get their work completed in the time allotted. These idealistic students may prefer to dream about becoming a Grade 3 teacher someday rather than working on the science project that is due tomorrow. You may have to monitor their time to keep them going.

The knowledge that they will have some **"personal" time** after their work is completed can go a long way to persuading them to use their allotted homework time wisely. Personal time may include screen time or time with friends and family. To encourage their children to get homework done early on Saturday afternoon one couple tells us that they often let them invite friends over for Saturday night at the movies. If the homework is not done the movie night is cancelled.

Getting There on Time for Resourceful Orange Learners

"Just-in-time" is how we would describe these learners when it comes to time management! That works for a short assignment handed to them one day for submission on the next day. However, it can work against them if they have a big assignment that they leave until the very last minute. It might mean they have to cancel some after school activities, or work much longer to complete it on time.

Help them **prioritize** the work that needs to be done in the time that they have allotted for homework. They may look at the pile of assignments as just too overwhelming. Or they may think they have to do it all "just in time" for tomorrow when, in reality, they may have more time than they think. Together, you can look at their agendas to decide what they need to do today. They may only need to concentrate on the drawing for health tonight, and then get the complete math assignment done for tomorrow.

Resourceful Oranges cringe when they are being monitored too closely. If you want to micromanage every homework assignment, please don't. Do take an interest, look at what they need to do and then give them some **space** in which to do it. Set a time when you are going to check on their progress, depending on their age of course, and then follow through.

Resourceful Oranges learn well if given **short deadlines**. Since they usually get their work done just in time, this might mean that you will have to step in and chunk their work to create shorter deadlines in order to get a huge project done in the long run. One parent outlined her method: "I have my child create an outline for an essay in two days, then research time for three days, then a draft in one week, etc. to make sure it is done on time." It helps them chunk the workload and work towards each short deadline. If they resist you can present it as a challenge.

Getting There on Time for Inquiring Green Learners

Timing can be problematic for Inquiring Green learners since time holds little relevance for them. They want time to discover and research the topic. You might want to help them learn to build in some extra **thinking time** for them to research, read, etc., to prepare their assignments. Otherwise, they may actually not get the work done by the deadline. They will often lament that there might just be one more tidbit to add before finally giving it up to the teacher.

As you may guess, these independent Inquiring Green learners want to research and learn in their own time and space. This sounds wonderful, but be cautioned that they may, in fact, only spend time on the subjects they think are important and disregard the others. **A little direction** goes a long way for these learners. One parent pointed out to us that her child will be working on his laptop, doing what she thinks is homework, but this child will be looking up fascinating information that has nothing to do with getting the work done for tomorrow.

They also dislike anything routine or repetitious which means they do not enjoy taking up time with **rote learning**. You may have to give them a nudge to learn the material anyway. They find it boring and one Inquiring Green learner wondered out loud why we would need to use up valuable time to memorize anything when all we have to do is look it up on the Internet! One way a mom told me she got around this notion that "repetition is boring" is she made a deal with her kid: learn the material and then you can have extra time to explore your interests.

The Reserved Learning Space

Reserved Learning Space for Organized Gold Learners: Guard Their Learning Area

Organized Gold learners want a **designated space** in which to do their homework, if only a little corner of a shared bedroom, family room or kitchen. They want it to be clean, tidy and efficient with "a place for everything and everything in its place!"

They are generally fastidious workers who keep a **meticulous** work space, no matter what their age. If they have siblings it is best to keep those siblings out of this work space, or at the very least, have them return everything to its rightful space.

They generally want **peace and quiet** in their orderly space. That may be difficult if they have siblings, but it is something to consider when you are looking for a space for Organized Gold learners. It may also be difficult if you set them up in the corner of the kitchen or the family room where chances are there is a television, a radio, or just a lot of family "noise" going on during their designated work time.

So what **tools** might be in their work space? A desk or table with a chair that is a good height for your child would be the first two things to set up. A lamp that provides good lighting is very helpful. They would prefer their own pencils, pens, markers, stapler, scissors, in a holder of some sort (it could even just be a favourite cup) that is sitting on the desk at arm's length. They would appreciate a shelf or two to hold their books, etc. Consider a docking station set up so they can place their devices in it before bed. You might want to think of providing a hook to hold their backpack so they know where to put it and where it is at all times.

Most important for the Organized Golds is the knowledge that their space is **safe and secure**. These are the kids who usually take really good care of their own belongings and want others to respect them as well. They may not have their own computer so sharing this with the family may be difficult for them, unless you set up a schedule so they know when they will have screen time. They guard their learning area.

Reserved Learning Space for Authentic Blue Learners: Study Where Their Heart Is

These very expressive children need to have expressive outlets, so some may play instruments, dance, paint, sculpt, etc. or just dream about doing some of these activities. One way you can create a nurturing learning space for them is by hanging pictures of them performing or of art relevant to them. If they love music, for example, let them choose pictures of musicians, dancers, or other artwork and display them throughout their space.

They enjoy communicating and self-actualizing, or just feeling they are improving daily. So hang relevant **quotes** and **posters** that have particular meaning to them in their space. Keep beloved books on their shelves. Change the books, the posters and the quotes as your Authentic Blues mature, find new interests, and evolve! In some cases these children have been known to read some of their favourite books over for years as they so often identify with some of the book characters, almost as if they are old friends.

Keeping the space **flexible** suits their flexible natures. For example, they may have enjoyed *The Cat in the Hat* series, or the *Harry Potter* books and are now reading different authors. Create posters from quotes you find on the Internet or in book stores or in art shops. One parent told us that her child's bedroom still had teddy bear wallpaper that had been expensive and she knew she should remove it. The lesson here is that you can change up posters, pictures, and books much easier than something as stationary as wallpaper.

Wherever they usually study, keep the space **cozy and informal**. They will enjoy a comfy chair to sit on when reading, although they might work at a table if they have a laptop and notes. They may prefer to sit at the kitchen table with you, with siblings, and/or with friends. They usually don't want to sit in a room by themselves doing homework. As one parent told us, she had a lovely bedroom set up for her child who only used it to store her books, etc., preferring to be in the family room working at a small coffee table while sitting in a big old chair. Just be sure to check with your child to see if a private space is important.

Reserved Learning Space for Resourceful Orange Learners: What Learning Space?

As you have likely guessed, these learners will get up and move around if they have been sitting for a while, or they may play with an object while sitting in one place. This active group usually has lots of fun things they wish to do and barely manage to squeeze the homework in between it all. Theirs is an **active environment** — a space filled with paraphernalia from their various activities, with their school books in the middle of everything. They tend to "grab what I need and go" as quickly as they can, and that includes when they rush out the door for school, hopefully with all of their homework!

"Tools" of preference for the tactile Resourceful Orange include items that appeal to all **five senses**. You may want to think about incorporating coloured paper, scented markers, audiovisual materials, and music in their learning spaces. These items might stimulate their senses so they would be more apt to use them to do homework.

They may use their "go-to" learning space more as a **place to store** everything they need. Their space will probably look disorganized to parents who are not of the Resourceful Orange persuasion! But your Resourceful Orange child will likely tell you something to the effect that "life is too short" or "it is just not fun to put everything in order." However, ask them if they can find a text book they need for the next day and they can usually produce it. One Resourceful Orange told me that they are organized — just not in the way in which society thinks of "organized" — and continued with this comment, "If I can find what I'm looking for then really what is the problem?"

Since they may not spend too much time in their actual learning space, chances are they will be doing their homework anywhere in the house. The more varied it is the happier they usually are. They may move from the kitchen table to the family room and then outside — all in one evening! We came up with the idea of having a little "tool" box filled with items they would need that they could take with them and act as a **workspace on the move.**

Reserved Learning Space for Inquiring Green Learners: Brains & Tech

These thinkers need space to ponder. They enjoy pondering theory, concepts, and a variety of subjects that interest them. They are curious about so many things that they just want the space in a day to wonder, "what if?" This may mean that they want a little space away from other family members so they are not disturbed in their thoughts.

They look for answers in reference books and on the Internet. Often they will think of the computer as a "best friend" since it holds so much of the knowledge that will satisfy their curiosity. While it is good that they will use the **computer** to explore a variety of topics, we caution you that this should not be at the expense of having real friends and a social life.

These children enjoy **collections**. It might be cars, stamps, rocks, coins, Lego, etc. Inquiring Green adults often tell us that not only did they collect items as children; they still have some of these collections. To encourage their quest for knowledge and their enjoyment of collecting items you may want to have a shelf that holds and displays their collections. It is a great way to build up their self esteem and make them feel good about their curiosity.

It has been said that if you just give an Inquiring Green a laptop and a place to sit down that will be their space for learning. They have amazing concentration levels when they are focused.

You now have some ideas that you can immediately put into action to help carve out a learning space that appeals to your kids, and thus inspire them to enjoy their journey as students. And as we head into the next chapter our know that you as parents will more fully appreciate the wonderful inborn natures of your children.

Chapter 9

CONCLUSION: THE FINAL GPS COORDINATES ARE YOURS!

Parents tell us over and over again that they know they only have this one opportunity to experience the parenting journey. They want it to be rewarding for them and for their children. They want to make the most of their time with their kids. They want to do the right things for their kids. At the end of our seminars many of these same parents tell us, often with tears in their eyes, that they now see how their parenting journey can become more exciting, more enjoyable, and more joy-filled. Armed with their new-found knowledge of how to help each one of their kids grow and develop their own respective skills and abilities, these parents feel like it is a journey of discovery they cannot wait to go home and continue!

With the magic of Disney in mind, you can apply the *GPS* strategies you have learned here to understand your children better, appreciate their strengths, talents and abilities and build stronger family relationships. We sincerely hope that your share of "bumps" will be few as you learn to use your radar detection. We trust that your family communication will flourish as you actively listen to what your kids say, and how they say it. And we are confident that you will engage your offspring more effectively as you recognize from where they draw their energy. As you do, you will join us in saying that parenting truly can be a "yummy" experience.

When we set out on this writing journey we wanted to share our joy of parenting, and now grandparenting, with you. We are confidant that you have picked up some of that joy and will be inspired to dig deep into the material to find the nuggets of gold that will help you on your journey towards an authentically happy family life with each and every one of your children.

GPS for Navigating Your Kid's Personality is a three-fold approach. It is this book which you now hold. It is also a series of workshops. It is also an opportunity for you to have one-on-one coaching or family coaching.

Our grandparenting role continues to evolve, just as your parenting role will, no doubt, as well. We would love to hear all about your "yummy" experiences as you incorporate *GPS* strategies into your parenting journey. If you have found some of these *GPS* strategies particularly effective as a parent, please do let us know. You can contact us at:

Kate@skills4people.com, or info@skills4people.com

www.skills4people.com

Enjoy Your Parenting Journey!

Enjoy Your Parenting Journey!

Resources

Chapter 1

1. Jung, Carl. (1976). *Psychological Types*. Princeton: Princeton University Press.

2. MBTI (Myers-Briggs Type Indicator) assessment is a psychometric questionnaire designed by Myers and Briggs to measure psychological preferences in how a person perceives the world and makes decisions.

3. Keirsey, D. (1998). *Please Understand Me II*. Del Mar, CA: Prometheus Nemesis Book Company.
   David Keirsey describes the four temperaments and the differences that distinguish each of them. It describes each one in depth and he uses the following titles: Guardians, Idealists, Artisans and Rationals. His book is considered to be one of the leading works on personality theory.

4. Don Lowry, a school teacher, inspired by the works of Jung, Myers-Briggs and Keirsey, developed True Colors, a visual and highly interactive way to introduce temperaments to students. Using four colours, Gold, Blue, Orange and Green, he combined fun and education to teach personal preferences and differences.

5. Berens, L.V. (2006). *Understanding Yourself and Others: An Introduction To The 4 Temperaments, 4.0.* Radiance House, Los Angeles, CA.
   Inspired by Jung, Myers-Briggs and Keirsey, Berens describes the differences in temperament such as core needs, values, abilities and behaviours. She defines the difference between our core self, our developed self and our contextual self.

6. Personality Dimensions® is a registered trademark of Career/ Life Skills Resources Inc., and is a Canadian tool developed by Career/Life Skills Resources Inc. over a five-year period. This tool relies heavily on earlier theorists as well as independent studies, and is a critical component of understanding yourself and others, and includes the Introvert/Extravert component. The descriptors used reflect the primary aspect of each of the four temperaments: Organized Gold, Authentic Blue, Resourceful Orange and Inquiring Green.

7. Tieger, P., and Barron-Tieger, B. (1997). *Nurture by Nature: Understand Your Child's Personality Type – and Become a Better Parent.* Toronto, ON: Little, Brown and Company. p. 15.

Chapter 2

1. Montgomery, S. (2002). *People Patterns: A Modern Guide to the Four Temperaments.* Del Mar, CA: Archer Publications.

2. Seligman, M. (2002). *Authentic Happiness.* New York, NY: Free Press.
   In his opening chapter Dr. Seligman introduces his readers to the notion of positive feeling and positive character so they will gain an understanding of what he means by authentic happiness.

3. Di Tella, Rafael; MacCulloch, Robert (23 June 2007). "Gross national happiness as an answer to the Easterlin Paradox?" *Journal of Development Economics* 86 (1): 22. doi:10.1016/j.jdeveco.2007.06.008. Retrieved 6 July 2013.

4. The Fordyce Emotions Survey. Michael Fordyce. Social Indicators Research 20, 335-381. Jan. 28, 2006.

5. Personality Dimensions® is a registered trademark of Career/LifeSkills Resources Inc. The PD at School booklet identified the core needs and a number of values for each temperament group.

6. Weil, A. (2011). *Spontaneous Happiness.* New York, NY: Little, Brown and Company p. 9.

7. Ibid.

8. Magic Kingdom® Theme Park Guidemap. New Fantasyland. Magic Kingdom® Theme Park provides guidemaps for each kingdom when you enter their parks. Also available as My Disney Experience app or visit MyDisneyExperience.com.

   http://en.wikipedia.org/wiki/Campbell's_Soup_Cans and http://ca.phaidon.com/agenda/art/articles/2013/february/22/the-fascinating-story-behind-andy-warhols-soup-cans/=

These sites provide information on Andy Warhol's soup can art.

Chapter 3

1. Coloroso, B. (2010). *Parenting Wit & Wisdom.* Toronto, ON: Penguin Group. p. 8-9.
   She also provides a full checklist for each of the 3 kinds of parenting (p. 10-13).

2. Keirsey, D. (1998). *Please Understand Me II.*
   Keirsey introduces the four icons for each of the temperaments in chapter 2, p. 20.

3. McGuiness, M. (2004). *You've Got Personality: An Introduction to the Personality Types described by Carl Jung & Isabel Myers.* Epping NSW, Australia: MaryMac Books.
   McGuiness sums each of the four temperament groups up in one word on page 11.

4. Keirsey, D. (1998). *Please Understand Me II.*
   Keirsey discusses parenting in chapter 8.

5. Montgomery, S. (2002). *People Patterns: A Modern Guide to the Four Temperaments.*
   Montgomery discusses parenting in chapter 4.

6. Ibid. p. 91.

Chapter 4

1. Keirsey, D. (1998). *Please Understand Me II.*
   Keirsey mentions Paracelsus in the chapters for each of his temperament group namely chapters 3, 4, 5 and 6.

2. Seligman, M. (2002). *Authentic Happiness.* New York, NY: Free Press. p. 245.

3. Personality Dimensions® is a registered trademark of Career/ LifeSkills Resources Inc. The PD at School booklet identified the strengths and abilities and likes (which we use for "the little engine that could" section) for each temperament group.

4. Seligman, M. (2002). *Authentic Happiness.* New York, NY: Free Press. p. 224.

5. Ibid. p. 224.

6. Career Dimensions™ ©2005 Career/LifeSkills Resources Inc. Career/LifeSkills Resources has conducted extensive research on the jobs that appeal to each temperament. Our listing of professions comes from their research.

7. http://www.peaceheroes.com/CraigKielburger/craigkielburgerbio.htm

8. Maddron, T. (2002). *Living Your Colors: Practical Wisdom for Life, Love, Work, and Play.* New York: Warner Books, Inc. p. 136.

9. Ibid. Chapter 4 on Blues.

10. Keirsey, D. (1998). *Please Understand Me II.* Keirsey talks about the Inquiring Greens in chapter 6 of his book. (indent at 10)

11. Montgomery, S. (2002), *People Patterns: A Modern Guide to the Four Temperaments.* Montgomery discusses Inquiring Greens in chapter 4.

Chapter 5

1. McGuiness, M. (2004). *You've Got Personality: An Introduction to the Personality Types described by Carl Jung & Isabel Myers.* page 10.

2. Berens, L.V. (2006). *Understanding Yourself and Others: An Introduction To The 4 Temperaments.* page 27.

3. Ibid. p. 27.

4. Personality Dimensions® is a registered trademark of Career/ LifeSkills Resources Inc. Our chapter on stress comes from a number of their resources; we chose the specific items that we felt would help parents understand their kid's stress the best. Sources included:
   - The Work-Life Balance Toolkit handout, "You'll know I'm stressed when I"
   - Colour Savvy: Helping You Achieve Success In Your Work Life, chapter 6.
   - Differentiated Instruction: Personality Dimensions and Learning Style.

5. Berens. p. 29.

6. Lee, D. (1974). *Alligator Pie*. Toronto, ON: Macmillan.

7. Maddron, T. *Living Your Colors: Practical Wisdom For Life, Love, Work, and Play.* p.39.

8. Ibid.

9. Ibid. p. 45.

10. Ibid. p. 44.

11. Ibid. p. 45

Chapter 6

1. Montgomery, S.(2002), *People Patterns: A Modern Guide to the Four Temperaments.* p. 72.

2. Keirsey, D. (1998). Please Understand Me II.
   In each of his chapters 3, 4, 5, and 6 he discusses how the temperaments communicate using the terms "words" (abstract and concrete); and "tools" (cooperative and utilitarian).

   Berens. L.V. (2006). *Understanding Yourself and Others: An Introduction To The 4 Temperaments.*
   On page 19-20 Berens uses the terms "words" (abstract and concrete), and "ways to interact" (affiliative and pragmatic).

   Montgomery, S.(2002), *People Patterns: A Modern Guide to the Four Temperaments.*
   In his chapter 4 he simplifies the discussion; we use his terms "words" (what is? and what's possible?), and "action" (what works? and what's right?).

3. http://www.pinterest.com/gardnermuseum/things-kids-say-about-art/
   This site illustrates how children talk about works of art.

4. Ibid.

5. Jones, Darlene E. (Kate) (1998). *Journal Writing: A Means to Self-Discovery. Brock Education: A Journal of General Inquiry.* 7 (2) Brock University Faculty of Education. P. 42-55.

6. Keirsey, D. (1998). *Please Understand Me II.*
   In each of his chapters 3, 4, 5, and 6 he discusses how the temperaments communicate using gestures.

   Personality Dimensions® is a registered trademark of Career/ LifeSkills Resources Inc. Our chapter on communication stems from a number of their resources; we chose the specific items that we felt would help parents understand their children's communication styles the best. Source included:

   Colour Savvy: Helping You Achieve Success In Your Work Life, chapter 7.

7. http://www.quotesworthrepeating.com/movie-quotes/mary-poppins-movie-quotes/

8. Keirsey. D. (1998). *Please Understand Me II*. p. 79 - 81.

9. Ibid. p. 78.

10. Jones, Darlene E. *Journal Writing: A Means to Self-Discovery*. p. 49.

11. Keirsey, D. (1998). *Please Understand Me II*. p. 80.

12. Geary, S. and Bulstrode, A. (2010). *Colour Savvy: Helping You Achieve Success in Your Work Life*. P. 107.

13. Keirsey, D. (1998). *Please Understand Me II*. p.120-122.

14. Montgomery, S. (2002), *People Patterns: A Modern Guide to the Four Temperaments*. p. 77.

15. Heinrichs, Ann (2006). *Similes and Metaphors: the magic of language*. Chanhassen, MN:The Child's World.

16. https://www.goodreads.com/work/quotes/1443553
This site has many quotes from Emily Dickinson's poems.

17. https://www.goodreads.com/author/quotes/875661.Rumi
This site has Rumi's quotes.

18. Jones, Darlene E. *Journal Writing: A Means to Self-Discovery*. p. 50.

19. Keirsey, D.(1998). *Please Understand Me II*. p.122.

20. Ibid. p. 36.

21. Geary, S. and Bulstrode, A. (2010). *Colour Savvy: Helping You Achieve Success in Your Work Life*. p 106.

22. Keirsey, D.(1998). *Please Understand Me II*. p.36.

23. Jones, Darlene E. *Journal Writing: A Means to Self-Discovery*. p. 52.

24. Keirsey, D.(1998). *Please Understand Me II*. p.36.

25. Ibid. P. 167-168.

26. htttp://web.mit.edu/invent/iow/low.html
This site describes Jeanie Lowten's invention, "The Kiddie Stool".

27. Shakespeare, Wm. *As You Like It*. Act II, Scene VII.

28. Heinrichs, Ann (2006). *Similes and Metaphors: the magic of language.*

29. Barton, M. (2012). *It's Raining Cats and Dogs: An Autism Spectrum Guide to the Confusing World of Idioms, Metaphors and Everyday Expressions*. Philadelphia, PA: Jessica Kingsley Publishers.

30. Keirsey, D. (1998). *Please Understand Me II*. p. 167.

31. Swanson, J. (2004). *Punny Places: Jokes to Make You Happy!* Minneapolis, MN: Carolrhoda Books, Inc.

32. Barton. M. (2012). *It's Raining Cats and Dogs: An Autism Spectrum Guide to the Confusing World of Idioms, Metaphors and Everyday Expressions.*

33. Jones, Darlene E. *Journal Writing: A Means to Self-Discovery*. p. 51.

34. Keirsey, D. (1998). *Please Understand Me II*. p. 168.

Chapter 7

1. Cain, S. (2013). *Quiet: The Power Of Introverts In A World That Can't Stop Talking.* NY: Random House, Inc. p. 3.

2. Tieger, P., and Barron-Tieger, B. (1997). *Nurture by Nature: Understand Your Child's Personality Type — and Become a Better Parent.* Toronto, ON: Little, Brown and Company.
   On page 15 the authors refer to introvert as "inny" and extravert as "outy".

3. http://blogs.disney.com/oh-my-disney/2014/04/14/what-is-your-disney-personality-type/?cmp=SMC%7Cblgomd%7COMDApril%7CFB%7CPersonality-OMD%7CInHouse%7C041414%7C%7C%7Cesocialmedia%7C%7C%7C
   This site suggests Disney characters that represent the sixteen personality types (as described in Myers-Briggs Type Indicator). Keirsey realized that within each of the temperament groups, four personality types fit, two of which are Introverts while the other two are Extraverts. We use this information to suggest a Disney character that fits the description for each of our vignettes.

4. Tieger, P., and Barron-Tieger, B. (1997). *Nurture by Nature: Understand Your Child's Personality Type — and Become a Better Parent.* p. 16.

5. McGuiness, M. (2004). *You've Got Personality: An Introduction to the Personality Types described by Carl Jung & Isabel Myers.* p. 3.

6. Cameron, C. (2009). *Splash: An Introvert's Guide to Being Seen, Heard and Remembered.* Concord, ON: Career/LifeSkills Resources, Inc. p. 12.

7. McGuiness, M. (2004). *You've Got Personality: An Introduction to the Personality Types described by Carl Jung & Isabel Myers.* p. 3.
8. Tieger, P., and Barron-Tieger, B. (1997). *Nurture by Nature: Understand Your Child's Personality Type — and Become a Better Parent.* p. 16.

9. Cain, S. (2013). *Quiet: The Power Of Introverts In A World That Can't Stop Talking.* p. 61.

10. Cameron, C. (2009). *Splash: An Introvert's Guide to Being Seen, Heard and Remembered.* Discussed on page 12.

    Cain, S. (2013). *Quiet: The Power Of Introverts In A World That Can't Stop Talking.* p. 10.

11. Ibid. Cain lists a number of introverts throughout her book.

12. Ibid.

13. Ibid. p. 10.

14. McGuire, W., and Hall, R.F.C. (1977) *Jung Speaking: Interviews and Encounters.* Princeton, N.J.: Princeton University Press, p. 304.

15. Tieger, P., and Barron-Tieger, B. (1997). *Nurture by Nature: Understand Your Child's Personality Type — and Become a Better Parent.* p. 15.

16. Cain, S. (2013). *Quiet: The Power Of Introverts In A World That Can't Stop Talking.* p. 3.

Chapter 8

1. Personality Dimensions® is a registered trademark of Career/ LifeSkills Resources Inc. This chapter comes from a number of their resources; we chose the specific items that we felt would help parents understand their offspring's needs for a home learning environment the best. Sources included:

   - Differentiated Instruction: Personality Dimensions and Learning Style.

2. Dunning, D. (2003). *Quick Guide to the Four Temperaments and Learning*. Huntington Beach, CA: Telos Publications. Dunning discusses these questions for each temperament group on p.23-26.

3. Keirsey, D. (1998). Please Understand Me

CPSIA information can be obtained at www.ICGtesting.com
Printed in the USA
BVOW06s1401180615

405219BV00004BA/8/P